That's How I Remember It!

Col B —

As I consider how the Lord authors our lives, I'm continually amazed and astonished with how He brings His children together to glorify Himself and bless us all.

Meant to be read aloud, my family stories are here for your enjoyment.

Thanks for your encouragement, leadership, fellowship and friendship, dear brother!

Blessings & His Love,

Ken

Ok, maybe it didn't happen exactly like that, but...

That's How I Remember It!

GROWING UP IN RURAL AMERICA

BY TOM KIMBALL

Ok, maybe it didn't happen exactly like that, but...

That's How I Remember It!

GROWING UP IN RURAL AMERICA

By Tom Kimball

www.TomKimball.com

The names and identifying characteristics of the folks featured
throughout the book have been changed to protect their privacy and dignity.
Any resemblance to actual persons, living or dead, is purley coincidental.

PUBLISHED BY

Firefish
BOOKS

publisher@firefishbooks.com

Library of Congress Control Number: 2011927134

ISBN 978-0-9835396-0-5

Book design by Alisa Hatcher
Story Editing by Heidi Kimball
Photographs by John F. Kimball, Sr., except where noted.
Cover Photos of Ethan Kimball by Ben Kimball

Manufactured in the United States of America
Third Edition

CONTENT

DEDICATION

To my wife, Tracey; my son, Benjamin and
his wife, Heidi; and to my magnificent
grandchildren, Megan, Ethan and Jack.
God makes life worth living...
you make the living worth telling.

ACKNOWLEDGMENTS

It takes a flotilla of dedicated and slightly "touched" people to make something like this little book a reality. Some call them Collaborators and others, Creative Partners. My mother might call them Conspirators. I call them family.

Art, like life, does not create itself in a vacuum. (In a vacuum cleaner perhaps, but not a vacuum. Which begs the question, 'How did the vacuum get dirty in the first place? And why am I the one cleaning it?' But I digress.)

What art *does* do is generate a creative vacuum which draws in other artists like lint to black cashmere. The bigger the vision, the bigger the suckage.

When I started writing these stories, I envisioned a series of humorous tales about growing up that would amuse and entertain; inspire and motivate; and provoke others to engage in their own storytelling.

Finally, it seemed like a fine idea to make a book. I'd made newspapers, I'd written articles and stories, I'd produced theatre, videos and television... how hard could producing a book be? About as hard as a kidney stone and not nearly as smooth.

But like any good producer/director, I know how to wrangle talent and get the best out of them in the process. So I assembled my team. Funny thing about that... they ended up wrangling me. They got the best out of me. And I am forever grateful.

Thanks to my best friend and wife, Tracey, who tirelessly challenged my grammar, encouraging me to aim higher and look more closely at every word on the page. Thanks, Honeyheart, for investing so much time in my vision.

To Ben, the brains and operations behind it all. Thanks for your persistence and discipline, son. Without your help my book would be like your refrigerator: a swarm of red and blue magnetic letters floating on a sea of white.

To Heidi, the delightful daughter I "inherited" from my son. Many thanks, Dear One, for the late-night, coffee-fueled writing sessions. What a story editor! You helped me hear my voice within the grammar. Couldn't have done it without you.

To Dad, who taught me how to work hard and work well. "Watch one. Do one. Teach one," he used to say. Thanks for taking all those snaps of the family. To Mom, whom I love and honor, thanks for getting me started off on the right foot. To Fil, who looks at his middle-aged brother and still sees the boy. Thanks for your fervent prayers over the years. To Alice, who taught me about friendship and loyalty... thanks for your love, sis. To my big sister, Susan, who went Home too young. I miss you still.

To Alisa Hatcher, our "daughter." Thanks for designing such an amazing platform for my little tome. You honor my work with your talent. Your work speaks for itself. (And makes me look better than my headshot.)

To everyone else — Rich Carvill, Lisa Coleman, Wayne Heus, John Kapinos, Kelly Mazezka, Justin Matott, Pamela McCreary, Dan McGowan, Steve Neff, David Priest, Rick Ramage, Brenda Rundback, Alex Strauch, Scott Ward, Kim Wheeler, Cindy Lee, the Carcirieri Family, and the dozens of others who read, edited, laughed, prayed, reminisced, and cajoled me to stay on course... many thanks!

The author and his son, Benjamin, on the
porch swing in Denver, Summer 1988.

FOREWORD

······················

A Child's Perspective

For as long as I've been alive my dad has been telling stories. Funny stories, mostly. To me at bedtime, to crowds in restaurants, clients in boardrooms, even the sick on their deathbeds. And until recently I didn't appreciate just how important that gift of storytelling could be. As it turns out, being a storyteller might just be one of the most important jobs on the planet. That said, I'm proud to say that MY dad — certainly in my mind the best storyteller in the world — is the author of this particular book of stories.

The first story of his childhood I can remember being told was his epic bike ride down Lyon Street.

I remember marveling that my brave dad — at just five years of age — had head-butted a fully-grown Gumball tree and lived to tell the tale. And while that might be the one I've heard him tell the most, my favorite story is the one about his first kidney stone.

(Both stories are in the book. You won't be disappointed.)

Honestly, I can't remember the first time he told me about the kidney stone, and when you read the account in this book I can neither confirm nor deny the accuracy of the quotes attributed to me. Frankly, I don't care. I prefer the story as it's written here. And as with any good story, a certain amount of embellishment has been added — where appropriate — for dramatic effect.

What I can say is that for as many times as I've heard him tell the story, I never get sick of hearing it. It's funny to me how the story changes each time it's told. About the third or fourth time I heard it, I stopped watching my dad as he told the story, and started to watch the audience.

In a group of old military buddies, there were a few more acronyms thrown in, and greater emphasis on the wild-eyed Air Force doctor. When he told it on a business trip to Vegas, the stone became a ball on a roulette wheel as dad won the 'jackpot.' Even though the details changed, every time he told it, it started and ended in the same place.

The reaction from the audience was likewise the same; the men would grunt, groan and moan in sympathetic agony. Everyone would breathe a sigh of relief as the pain subsided; with the impending doom at the prospect of the crazy doctor 'going in after it,' they'd be on the edge of their seats.

Without fail the audience would practically cheer with him when he passed the stone, secretly rejoicing to themselves, "I've passed the stone!" Somewhere in the middle of the story he had *connected* with them. Connected so deeply that they had put *themselves* into the story.

Isn't that what makes the best stories 'the best?' We read *Treasure Island* and believe *we* are Jim Hawkins stranded on an island battling pirates. We read *Lord of the Rings* and believe *we* are Frodo and we must destroy the ring!

While the stories in this book may not be quite as fantastical as those I've mentioned above, it is my hope that they do for you what they've always done for me: take you back to a simpler time — childhood — when the world was uncomplicated, and the biggest real-life problem you had was the dog that chased you on your paper route.

Lastly, I'll advise you of the following. The stories in this book are meant to be shared. Aloud. With other people. If you've never read a story aloud before, this book is a great place to start. There is something about reading words aloud that breathes life into a story.

Sharing stories with others is part of what makes our lives worth living. Some of the stories in this book may seem too fantastic to be true. They probably are.

So if my Dad's memory of his life — mixed with a healthy dose of imagination — can bring a smile to your face, does it really matter what's fact and what's fiction?

That's how I want to remember it. I'll bet that you do, too.

Benjamin R. Kimball

The author on duty at his public affairs desk with the 48th Tactical Fighter Wing while stationed at RAF Lakenheath, Suffolk, England, from 1980 - 83.

PREFACE

·····················

Kidney Stones & Cocoa Puffs

I was eating breakfast with my son, Benjamin, some years ago when he was nearly seven. I was eagerly describing to him the time an Air Force doctor treated me for a kidney stone at Fort Ord Army Hospital.

It was January of 1980, and as an enlisted airman I was studying Russian at the Defense Language Institute on the Presidio of Monterey in California.

"You have to understand the times," I said to Ben, as we ate our Cocoa Puffs, "this was during the Cold War."

"What's a cold wart?" he asked, trying to sound serious.

"The Cold War, son. It was a war that wasn't really a war. We just pretended like it was to keep from actually having a real one."

He chewed thoughtfully. "You mean like a cold that really isn't the flu, but that's what you tell everyone so you can stay home from work and watch movies with me?"

Smart kid. "Yeah, something like that. Only I got a medal."

"You got a medal for watching movies? Cool." Did I mention Ben also inherited my sense of humor?

I explained that while we constantly trained for war, we had not actually fought in one. And it made us all just a little nuts, I think. It was kind of like kissing your arm to practice for that first big date with the amazing blond from chemistry class, but then never having the opportunity to actually kiss her.

"Yuck. You kissed your arm?" That he didn't get. He would... in time. I knew I might have to explain the Cold War again later, but Ben seemed satisfied for the moment. He crunched attentively.

"Anyway, I had this Air Force doctor assigned to my case who was more than a little odd," I mused. "It was like he declared war on my kidney stone."

"What's a kidney stone?"

"It's a stone that forms in your kidneys like a pearl in an oyster," I said, explaining briefly how kidneys work.

"Why?"

"I don't know, son. The doctors don't know. The oysters don't know. Nobody knows. It's a mystery."

"Sounds cool. Can I do that?"

"You won't want to after you hear what happened to me."

I continued my story, explaining that this Marine-wannabe was determined to leave no stone unturned, so to speak, and that this was very worrisome to me since the stone he was romancing was mine.

"After two days of painkillers, I still felt a burning sensation when I tried to relieve myself: like pushing a fireball of molten razor blades through my, well, uh, you know, my personal business. Nothing came out but a trickle." Ben stopped crunching.

"Through your tooter?" he asked, waiting intently for my answer. (It's a long story, but "tooter" is what we named his "boy business" when he was about two... something to do with chili for dinner and a bubble bath later and fragrant bubbles and a song about musical fruit... well, you get the picture.)

I nodded. He squeezed his eyes shut. *That* he understood.

I went on to explain, however, that on the morning of the third day, I experienced my own private resurrection: the pain was completely gone. I believed that my kidney stone had been miraculously rolled away. Cast aside! Vanquished!

That evening I told the doctor I felt better and asked when I could go home. That's when that crazy look washed over his face again like shower steam on a bathroom mirror.

He turned to me and out of his doctor's lips oozed those dreadful words that no man ever wants to hear: "The reason you don't feel any pain is because the stone has stopped moving. If you don't pass that stone by tomorrow morning, we're going to have to go in after it!"

Go in after it? How in the world would you go in after a kidney stone, I thought to myself?

"Excuse me, sir? What exactly does that mean: 'go in after it?'"

No response.

"Uh, sir?"

Dr. Commando snapped his head to the left, his neck cracking chiropractically. He slowly turned back to face me.

"There are only two ways to go in, Airman Kimball," he said, whispering so close I could smell the Brut aftershave. "The first is to find the stone by x-ray then fillet open your plumbing and pluck it out."

"Sir? You're scaring your Airman."

I sat up, looking into his eyes for some reasonable facsimile of a human being. I understood surgery but the other way was, well, unthinkable.

"What's the other way?"

"The other way, Airman," said the young captain, "involves this stainless steel cable with a tiny yet powerful claw at one end." His eyes grew distant and I could see that he was running the procedure over in his mind. He became more animated as he went on, using his hands to demonstrate.

"After you insert the cable you run it up as far as necessary until you find the stone. You then grab the stone... " He picked up an empty Styrofoam cup, "...and crush it." The cup was reduced to plastic snowflakes.

"Insert the cable... where?" I asked the doctor, not really wanting to know.

I was breaking into a sweat remembering.

"Where, Daddy?"

I looked at Ben. "You know where."

Ben mouthed the word "tooter?"

I nodded.

"Then as quickly as the doctor appeared, he was gone," I said, watching Ben's face. "I could see him darting from corner to corner down the hall in the hospital like he was on some secret mission.

"My heart and mind were racing. Ok. So he was going to use force. He was, after all, a military doctor. He understood the use of deadly force. No biggie. And, of course, this was an Army hospital. Lots of soldiers. I was attending a top secret intelligence school. I could handle it. Maybe this was how they recruited for the CIA...

"Now, son," I said, "this was the best part. You would have been proud of your old Dad." I puffed up my chest and held my spoon so he could see the lone Cocoa Puff in it. He had finished eating, so I had his complete attention.

"I displayed the same courage any man would when another threatens his, uh, 'tooter' with a razor-sharp instrument."

"How's that, Daddy?"

"Well, son," I said, "I prayed like a tuna being chased by a shark."

"Did God hear you?"

"Actually, I think everyone in Southern California did. At my midnight potty break the night before the invasion, I had to pee so bad my back teeth were floating. I pushed and pushed against the pressure until—aauugghh!—I shrieked in utter agony and passed the stone into the center of the strainer."

At that, I dropped the Cocoa Puff into his empty bowl for effect. It rolled around the rim and was halfway around the bowl before dropping into the center of a small milk puddle. Ben's eyes were focused on the Cocoa Puff. He shuddered.

I picked up his bowl and walked around the kitchen, reenacting the moment.

"I gripped the strainer, like this, and with the other hand I grabbed my IV stand and I scurried down the hall. I announced to anyone and everyone that the surgery scheduled in the next few hours would not be necessary: 'I passed the stone! I passed the stone! I passed the stone!'"

I put the bowl back in front of my son. He was wide-eyed, looking at me, then the bowl. "Daddy! A Cocoa Puff came out of your tooter? Wow! Wait'll I tell my friends!" He ran out of the room.

Perfect. I was a hero. His mother was going to kill me.

She called the next day.

"What in the world did you tell Ben?"

"Why? What's the problem?" I held my breath.

"He won't eat his cereal without shouting 'I passed the stone! I passed the stone!' between every bite."

See, that's the challenge with being a storyteller. If there isn't some embellishment here and there, some of life's important moments are too easily forgotten. There's really no point to telling a story unless it's memorable.

I attempted to explain that to my son's mother.

So. Enjoy these stories. They're all absolutely true... at least, that's how I remember it.

Tom Kimball

PART 1

· · · · · · · · · · · · · · · · · · · ·

To begin with...

Photo by Tom Kimball

Eerie and silent, McConnell's Haunted House as seen from a bedroom
window in the author's home near Havre de Grace, Maryland, circa 1970.

CHAPTER 1

• • • • • • • • • • • • • • • • • • • •

McConnell's Haunted House

"It's got me! Tommy, help! Billy! I can't breathe!"

What happened next can only be explained as unbelievable. I don't know if it was the fact we were the first people in the house in decades or if there really was a ghost lurking in the basement, but back in the corner, something fell. Something big and heavy and angry.

Oh. Sorry. I'm getting ahead of myself.

Living in the country offers even the meekest explorers more than ample opportunity for escapades right outside your back door. And our neighbor's farm to the west was a spectacularly rich land of adventures just waiting to be dreamed, imagined and discovered.

Almost one hundred times the size of our nearly one-acre parcel, McConnell's dairy farm was partly woods, partly pasture, partly corn and alfalfa—and mostly a land of, well, milk and honeysuckle.

Our property sat smack in the middle of the eastern-most border of the farm along McConnell's Creek. Massive oak trees stood sentry on either side of the creek's entire length. These ancient branches, lifting their acorns more than a hundred feet in the air, were joined by scores of smaller deciduous brothers: cedar, sycamore, beech, gum, maple, wild cherry, dogwood, and sassafras trees. No doubt some of these mighty arbors were mere

3

saplings when Abraham Lincoln spoke at a memorial in a little place called Gettysburg, not far from my home.

In the late 1950s and early Sixties, McConnell kept dozens of dairy cows. In the summer the cows congregated in the creek bed and under the trees to beat the heat, munch on the undergrowth, drink their fill, and make cow patties.

When we were really young, we'd hang out by the fence and hand-feed the cows some of the long, luxurious grass that grew in our yard. It was endlessly entertaining to tease the heifers with the grass, each of us trying to get his or her animal to stick her tongue out the farthest. We'd giggle, watching them struggle to stretch their necks over the barbed wire fence, eyes bulging, big wet cow noses glistening with cow snot, grasping at the gourmet greens we held in our hands. There's something very calming about a cow eating out of your hand.

Cows are definitely cool and not at all scary... which is why it surprised me to discover a haunted house on McConnell's Farm.

The house was a quarter mile south of the main farmhouse. After the leaves fell in the fall and until they filled out again in the late spring, I could see the house from my bedroom window. It was a gray and unpainted two-story affair nestled at the edge of the Far Wood to the west.

Someone must have died a horrible death there, which is why the house now stood empty and mournful—no color, no windows, no life left in it, nothing but forgotten, painful moments in time. Perhaps a farm worker from a previous century and a far-away country. This particular Saturday afternoon in the spring of 1966, the old house called out to me.

"It's haunted," said Billy Wheats, the neighborhood expert on absolutely everything. He held my father's binoculars like they were his. "We should check it out." Yeah, right. Like I was going to believe anything Billy said about ghosts and haunted houses. Having the best Halloween costume every year didn't make him an expert on the hereafter.

Dad was working in the yard. He'd know if it was haunted. I walked over while Billy kept an eye on the old house.

"The old tenement behind McConnell's barn?" Dad asked,

tamping the earth around a newly transplanted scrappy azalea with his shoe. He knew which house I meant. "Why do you think it's haunted?"

"Billy says it is." Dad smiled.

"Could be, I suppose." Dad didn't look up but scooped another shovelful of dark earth and deftly tossed it around the main stalk of the plant in one even motion. "Never know what's buried anywhere, unless you put it there yourself."

Billy sauntered up. "Hey, Mr. Kimball."

"Billy."

Dad suddenly stopped and crouched down next to the bush and peered over it, raising a curious eyebrow. He stared at the freshly turned earth closest to me. I knelt down. I couldn't see what he saw but knowing my father, there was some object lesson in all of this. I followed his gaze to the base of the azalea.

I got down on my hands and knees and brushed some of the dirt aside, close to the bush. Billy couldn't stand the suspense.

"What? What are you doing, Tommy?" He cocked his head trying to figure out what was going on between Dad and me. "What do you see?

Something shiny caught my eye. "Treasure," I said, pulling out a brand new, Kennedy half-dollar from the dirt. Dad looked at me with that imperceptible smile that only those of us who knew him could see. "Imagine that," he said, and walked away.

I looked at the half dollar. "Thanks, Dad." He waved a 'you're welcome' over his shoulder. I jammed the coin into the watch pocket of my jeans as I stood.

"How'd he do that?" Billy asked, getting up. "Why'd he do that?"

"Don't you see, Billy? It's a secret code. Dad was trying to tell me that there's buried treasure in McConnell's Haunted House." This news, of course, was music to Billy's ears. His father was the town jeweler. Treasure was something that Billy understood. And, being the biggest (tallest, largest, roundest) kid our age in the neighborhood, he was the perfect sidekick for a skinny super hero like me.

"Treasure? Let's go get it!" Billy shouted impulsively. The lad was fiercely loyal to adventure but not very quiet.

"Shhh! We need to talk about this somewhere else." I ran to the way-back yard and my secret hideout in the patch of sassafras trees just beyond the leach field and bamboo. Billy could hardly keep up. He wasn't much of a runner. We huddled in the lean-to fort I made from a drawing in my Dad's book on surviving in the wilderness.

"I know what we need to do this," I said, having read every Hardy Boys Mystery at least twice... a month.

"What? A flashlight? I've got a backpack to carry the gold. How about a pick? I have an old Army foxhole shovel. Don't you have an axe... you know, to chop down the door? And for zombies, in case your gun jams and we can't shoot our way out?"

Billy was flushed with excitement, his eyes wild. How could you not love a guy like that? Yeah, he was my best friend. Zealous and sincere, a perfect follower. He needed a leader. He needed me.

"Ok, great ideas, Billy. But first, we need another guy. Someone small enough to get into places we can't."

"Smaller than you?"

I stared at him. Really? "Who're you calling small?"

Billy grinned. He loved being big. And he knew what, or rather who, I was talking about.

"Wilson?"

"Wilson."

"Oh man, he's such a baby. You know he's just going to complain the whole time. And what about Patty? What if she finds out? She'll beat us all up and take the gold."

"Billy... first, we don't know if there's anything in that old house except some dead coons and bats in the attic. Besides, we need him to go first."

This, Billy understood. He may have been the biggest kid in our neighborhood, but he was not big on being brave.

We laid out our plan: who was going to bring what, when we were going, and what we were going to do with any treasure we found. Billy went home, picking up Wilson on the way back.

They came back an hour later, both carrying backpacks, tools in hand, ready to explore.

I looked up through the budding trees at the sun. It was hazy, hanging in the sky a few hours above tree line. It would be light long enough for us to get in, but would it be light long enough for us to get out?

Missy looked up at me with her brown canine eyes. She knew something was up. I scratched behind her ears as Billy and Wilson walked up, acting nonchalant and looking obvious. I hitched Missy to her dog run and the three of us headed out.

The best place to cross the fence was by the dogwoods where the barbed wire was stretched and rusted out. We crossed the creek and hiked due west to the rock pile. From the cover of the rocks we had an unobstructed view of the haunted house. Farmer McConnell was working near the barn that was about a hundred yards farther along on the other side of the house from where we were. We waited for him to go inside before breaking cover and making a low run to a clump of trees between the house and us.

Once we were in the trees we put the house between the barn and us and sprinted to the house. It was L-shaped, with what looked like a smaller room attached to the larger, older, A-frame structure. I got there first with Wilson right on my heels. Billy trundled in a couple of minutes later, panting and sweating enough for all of us. We huddled on the small porch.

He started to speak but I held up my hand. The sound of the tractor starting sent a chill up my spine. I'd met Mr. McConnell once with my Dad. There was a hole in the side of his mouth where he clenched a pipe, his beard yellowed from the smoke. His hands were large and rough. His broken fingernails were black with the stains of working around cows and crops and crud...at least eight of them were. He was missing half his left index finger. His left thumb was entirely gone. A hungry piece of farm machinery, no doubt. Or worse...

"Oh man, I think he saw us! We are in such trouble!" whined Wilson.

"Shut up, Wilson!" Billy squeezed Wilson's head, pinching it like a bowling ball.

"Ow! That hurt, Billy! I'm telling Patty!"

"You do and I'll squash you like a bug."

"Will you two stop it!" I couldn't take it any more. "Stay here."

I crawled to the corner of house to get an idea of which direction he was headed. I pressed the eyepieces to my head. I couldn't see him but the sound of tractor was getting closer. I dropped the binoculars to get a bead on him without the glass. He was halfway to the haunted house.

I ran back to the porch. "He's coming right for us!"

"Oh man, I knew it!" Wilson stood up. Billy pulled him back down.

"What are you doing? Get down!" Billy looked at me. "Ok chief, what next?"

I looked back at our escape route. We'd never make it to the trees before McConnell saw us. We couldn't hide around the house; there was no cover.

"We gotta get inside," I said, half to myself.

"What? Are you crazy? We don't know what's in there!"

"Got no choice. We came here to find treasure. The only thing we can do is break in and hide before McConnell gets here."

Wilson was backing out. "I'm not going in."

The tractor chugged closer. "Well, I'm not staying here just to get shot."

Billy heard me. "What makes you think he'll shoot us?"

I held up the binoculars and lied. "He's got a rifle." With that, I reached into my pack and pulled out my hand axe. I threw the bag over my shoulder and went to what appeared to be a back door. Like my hero Andy Hardy, I thwacked the door once and nothing. I hit it hard again the second time and much to my surprise the whole door fell into the house.

McConnell's tractor bearing down on us left no time to enjoy the moment. He shifted gears or something. We bolted into the house through the open doorway. Without a word, we all picked up the door and worked it back into the opening. Billy and Wilson held it in place while I looked for a way to brace it.

McConnell's tractor chugged closer and closer, stopping just thirty feet or so from the house where we had just been hiding.

The tractor idled patiently, neutral to the unfolding drama.

The old house creaked as I tiptoed across the kitchen with a loose board from the old pantry. The sound of McConnell's engine covered the noise of jamming the board under the doorknob. Then it suddenly stopped; the only sound now was a faint hum and Billy's wheezing.

I peeked through a gap between the door jam and the wall that years of neglect and woodland creatures had created. McConnell was off his tractor and headed to the door!

"He's coming this way!" I whispered. Billy turned white. Wilson swore. And my adrenals dumped enough juice into my system that I'm certain I could have taken on the old farmer single-handed.

"Quick! Lean on it!" All three of us pressed our elementary school bodies against the door. McConnell walked up the two steps and tried the handle. We stopped breathing. He tried it a second time. With a humpf, apparently satisfied that all was secure, he walked back to his tractor and drove off.

I'm not really sure how long we stayed there holding that door up, probably only a few minutes, but it seemed like hours.

Wilson was the first to whisper hoarsely. "What's that humming?"

Billy and I, both a year older and wiser, looked at each other, then at Wilson, and fell on the floor, laughing. Wilson never liked anyone laughing at him. He picked up an old can or something from the counter and threw it at us. We saw it coming and ducked. But what happened next, none of us saw coming.

Wilson's 8-year-old arm was strong but not accurate. His throw sent the can into what must have been a pantry but was now home to wasps. I'm not really sure what kind but there were plenty of them. And they were understandably upset that someone had thrown a can into their living room; they didn't really care who they stung in the process of blowing off a little steam.

Retreat to the safest place — outside — was effectively blocked by our earlier efforts, so we had no choice but to seek refuge in other parts in the house. (Important safety tip when running from wasps: don't run upstairs. Besides stinging, wasps love to fly. Upward. It's all about a tactical advantage.)

Up the stairs we went to one of the two bedrooms on the second floor that still had a door. Once safely inside, we figured all we had to do was a wait a few minutes, maybe half an hour, and we could sneak past the wasps and get out of the house. Treasure hunting was no longer a priority.

Actually it takes a lot longer than that for wasps to settle down. Much, much longer. The afternoon slipped away while we all waited around on the old wooden floors. Wilson was as mad as the wasps but didn't say anything since he was the one who threw the can. Billy, on the other hand, asked me what I thought about the people who used to live there.

So I told him what I thought. What I didn't know about the family — which was a lot — I just made up. (It kept our minds off of the wasps.) You know, imagining what they must have been like, moving into the house right after the Civil War. The father had been killed at Gettysburg but his wife had remarried McConnell's great-great granddaddy, a mean old cuss who was deaf in one ear, no teeth save one eye tooth that stared out of his always opened mouth, and a bad limp from a Yankee bullet he still carried in his hip since Shiloh.

I loved the Civil War. My family traveled to the Manassas National Battlefield Park on July 21, 1961 to witness the first, and as it turned out, the only reenactment of a Civil War battle at a national park.

The First Battle of Bull Run was probably as chaotic as the reenactment. Even though I was only four-years-old, I remember it vividly: smoke everywhere, cannons booming, rifles cracking, men running every which way, the yelling and shouting… and that was just the line for the latrine.

What I remember most was how angry Pop was with my big brother who went and got himself lost for six hours. I reckon he was lucky Dad didn't leave him, and lucky to see his sixteenth birthday 10 days later.

So, spinning a yarn about a Civil War family, true or not, was just as natural to me as it was natural for an angry raccoon — who unexpectedly appeared out of the wall — to rear up on her hind legs and give chase to her perceived enemy... namely me.

After yanking the door off its hinges, Billy, screaming like a wild cat, lunged down the stairs. Wilson made the mistake of trying to go first and the two boys half tumbled, half ran, down the stairs, landing in a heap of cursing and squealing kids. I slipped past them only to discover that the raccoon ruckus had only aggravated the wasps again.

Our last hope to outrun the assault was to retreat to the basement where, of course, the ghosts lived. All of them. In the universe. At least that's what Billy said as I opened the door and we crammed onto the top step. Billy closed the door.

The simple stairs of ancient, gray wood, unfinished and splintered, led down to an unusually dry dirt floor. The single room was just deep enough for an average man to stand upright. The stone walls curved as if being pushed in from the other side. A mud-caked, single-pane window allowed a solitary shaft of afternoon sunlight to stab the old basement with an eerie, dusty glow.

Wilson called out to me. "What do you see? Anything?"

"Nothing," I said, "Nothing, except... " I let my voice trail off as I dug out my flashlight. "Wait. What's this... ?" I walked away from the bottom of the steps so neither boy could see me.

Billy, who held the door closed behind him to stave off the incoming wasps, now stood in abject terror at the top of the steps, too afraid to move. Wilson sat down and watched me creep into the darkest corner of the basement.

I could barely contain my delight. A devious plan formed in my head especially with all that we had been through: Farmer McConnell, the wasps, the rabid raccoon; and now the basement of a real haunted house? Scaring my little sister was always satisfying, but this... how could I pass up this opportunity?

My mind raced to build a convincing story. "What's this in the ground here? Something, wooden... " I asked casually. I made some digging noises.

Wilson couldn't resist. "What? Wooden? What do you see?" He crept down a little farther, far enough to see my silhouette against the light of my flashlight on the floor. "What is it, Tommy?" He made his way down the stairs, digging for his flashlight.

"I dunno… something half buried," I said, shining the light down into the dirt. Wilson clicked on his light and scurried over to me.

"It looks like there's something in there." I continued.

Wilson peered over my shoulder. "Move. Lemme see." I put a finger to my mouth, urging him not say anything else and follow my lead.

"See?" I said for Billy's benefit. "What do you suppose that is?" I held the flashlight to my face and then whispered to Wilson. "A box." I pointed to where Billy stood at the top of the stairs. Wilson grinned. *Scare the big kid. Got it.*

"Tommy? Wilson? What's going on, guys? What do you see?"

"There's an old wooden box," Wilson piped up. I smiled approvingly.

"Yeah, but it looks really heavy, and half buried. Can't move it. Bring the shovel down here and let's dig it out." I said, adding to our evolving ghost story.

"What's in it?" Billy stood firm.

"We have to dig it out, first," I said, building the suspense. "Can you give us a hand?"

"What's it look like?" Billy was not going to be easily convinced.

"Looks like a treasure chest or something." Wilson said impatiently. I frowned at him. A treasure chest? Seriously? Billy won't buy that. I flicked Wilson's ear.

"No," I said, "It's more like an old tool chest." I grabbed Wilson and led him silently along the long wall back to where the stairs jutted into the basement. We stopped directly under the steps on which Billy stood. We crouched in the shadows.

Wilson was having a hard time stifling his glee (and his over-acting). "Tommy, look, it's opening by itself!"

"What?!" Billy squeaked.

Ok, so maybe this was working after all.

"Shut up, Wilson! It's not opening. That's just a shadow." I said, disguising my snicker as a gasp of fear. I pulled Wilson in close and grabbed his shirt collar with both hands. Wilson clenched his neck down on my hands and pretended I was choking him.

His voice wheezed. "It's got me! Tommy, help! Billy! I can't breath!" I pulled my hands away. Wilson and I fell apart, barely containing our laughter. Wilson coughed to cover. I groaned. Billy whimpered.

What happened next can only be explained as unbelievable. I don't know if it was the fact we were the first people in the house in decades or if there really was a ghost lurking in the basement, but back in the corner, something fell. Something big and heavy and angry.

Whatever revenge Wilson planned to exact on Billy was now forgotten. We directed our lights into that corner where only moments ago we imagined a wooden box; two shining eyes reflected the light back to us, and in an instant, the entire stone wall corner collapsed in a cloud of rock and dust.

Our collective adrenalin spike caused us both to scream like girls at a Beatles concert. Billy, now maintaining a continuous deafening shriek, bolted down the stairs. Midway down the hundred-year-old staircase, a step gave way, and Billy's leg shot through, nearly clobbering both of us in the face. Dropping my flashlight with a shout, I instinctively tackled the dangling appendage and hung on.

Billy, of course, tried to pull his leg back out, thinking that whatever had "killed" me and Wilson now had a firm hold on him. I let go but the broken board had snagged his leg at the knee. The more he pulled, the more the steps groaned and the more hysterical Billy became.

"Let go! Let. Go. Of. ME!" and with one, last mighty pull Billy jerked his leg free and tumbled down the remaining steps, leaving a huge chasm between us and the way out.

We all panted and whimpered quietly for what seemed an eternity. I picked up a nearby flashlight and with a shaking hand shined it back into the demon-possessed corner. On top of the pile of rocks in the corner was... a dead opossum. Well, I'm not sure he was dead, but we didn't stay to find out.

"You guys okay?" I asked. They nodded. I looked at the

window. If we climbed halfway back up the stairs we could probably crawl out through the opening.

"Let's go home," I said, and started up the stairs. As I passed Billy, he kicked me in the backside.

"Your shorts are ripped." I pulled them around and looked. And just as I looked, we had one last unexpected surprise. I'm guessing now, looking back, that it was because I was relieved and no longer screaming. I let out a long, musical toot.

Of course we started laughing. Hysterically. The giggles reached fever pitch when Billy got stuck in the window, with Wilson on the outside pulling, and me on the inside pushing. I reckon we were only there a few minutes, but boy, did that laughter feel good.

So, no ghosts, no hidden treasure, and only a few scratches and bruises. I'm certain if you were to sit them both down and ask them to recollect what happened that day, they'd each tell you the same thing I'm telling you now: "Ok, maybe it didn't happen exactly like that, but that's how I remember it."

CHAPTER 2

● ● ● ● ● ● ● ● ● ● ● ● ● ● ● ● ● ● ●

Climbing a Tree With My Bike

It was thrilling. I had to tell someone; so I asked my little sister, who was just four, to sit on the front porch and watch. Yeah. Even then I needed an audience.

Even though 1962 was a long time ago, I remember distinctly figuring out how to ride a bike by myself. I couldn't learn fast enough. I didn't use training wheels—we couldn't really afford them and Dad simply didn't believe in them—so I trained in the back yard on the grass.

Like most kids growing up in rural Maryland in those days, I was more interested in getting a bike than almost anything else. Riding a bike was more than a rite of passage; it was freedom. Even though I was only starting kindergarten in the fall, I knew that if I learned to ride a bike early I would be free to come and go like the big kids.

Of course, the Sixties were replete with cool bicycles and awesome accessories to trick them out: chopper handlebars, banana seats, handgrips with tiger heads and streamers, reflectors, lights, generators, bells, horns, etc.

It seemed like every kid in the neighborhood that year— except me—was getting a new bike. My dad told me he was going to get me a bike, but not a new one. My father was pretty handy with things like that. As promised, midsummer he came home with a two-wheeler…a fixer-upper. It was bittersweet and

I think he saw the disappointment in my eyes.

"Don't worry, we'll fix 'er up. She'll be the fastest bike in the neighborhood," he said.

And with that, he set about refurbishing this small but sturdy bike he picked up at the junkyard for a few dollars. She was a squatty, 20-inch, boy's bike without fenders. In his basement workshop we sanded off all the rust, tightened up the spokes, packed new grease in the hubs, and put a new seat on her. We then mounted new, fat tires with some heavy tread and puncture-proof tubes, a new foot brake, and new hand grips.

Finally, we painted her black. It was the only color we had. She was gorgeous. Actually, as I think about it, *we* didn't do any of those things; Dad did all of them.

Blackie would be my best friend on the roads around the neighborhood for the next five years or so, until my paper route and I outgrew her. At first, I didn't realize how cool my bike was until some of the other kids who could ride better than me kept asking to borrow her. Blackie was fast and surefooted, on and off the road. I'm certain the trail bikes of today can be traced to her lineage.

Anyway, I could see how amazing it would be to be able to get out and ride her fast and furious. I couldn't wait to do that.

So I practiced riding circles in the lawn. Balancing, turning, and stopping. I was getting proficient at all of them. And yeah, maybe just a little cocky.

Just before school began, I started making short solo runs on Lyon Street. Slowly I gained confidence, riding a few dozen feet at a time, then stopping, heart racing, almost ready to jump from the nest; riding a few more feet the next time, a little farther, a little faster.

Our house sat at the dead end of Lyon Street, on the edge of McConnell's farm. It was not the traditional, lollipop cul de sac you find in suburbs all over America today; it was a true dead end. (Which was really only partially true. In many ways it was a "live end" with several large gum and sycamore trees dug in deep.)

While I was growing up, smack dab in the middle of that

dead end, a huge white oak towered over the street and all the other trees on the border of the farm. So when I summoned the courage to ride on the street, I tackled a few feet at a time. I'd ride my bike up the street maybe a dozen feet, turn around and drift back into the safety of our front yard. One weekend, I was particularly brave and managed several runs of the entire block, from the mailboxes to our front porch.

"Hey, Alice! Watch this!" I rode halfway up the block and turned around. I wanted to be sure my little sister could see me. I coasted the bike down the street, into and across our drive, and up to the front porch.

"Pretty neat, huh?" I said.

She shrugged her shoulders. "Kinda slow."

"N'uh-uh. Watch this." I took off again, turned around halfway up the block and pedaled some speed into my run this time. This time I zipped across the yard and skidded to a stop, kicking up some dust.

Alice was on her feet. Clapping. That's all the encouragement I needed. Just then, Susan walked out onto the porch.

"What're you up to?" she said, plopping down next to where Alice was standing.

"Riding. Wanna see?"

"Sure!"

So off I went, on my third run, confidence building, feeling pretty good about myself.

During this whole exhibition, a little voice of reason spoke my father's words in my head. *Take it easy. Take it slow.*

So off I went, nice and easy, nice and slow. This time I coasted into the drive before braking, making a big show of stopping in the dirt just in front of my adoring fans. Again, applause, which, I presume, attracted my big brother.

Being the big man on the campus, he wasn't so impressed with my riding skills. He'd won some statewide, car-driving award for teenagers. Not sure what he did to win, he was kind of a nerd; but hey, that's cool. He got some giant trophy out of it.

"What's going on?" he asked.

"Tommy is showing us how well he can ride Blackie down

the hill from the mailboxes," Susan said.

"Just the mailboxes?" Fil said. "Shoot, that's only a block. What about from the bus stop?"

"You don't have to ride that far, Tommy." Susan gave Fil one of those "looks" sisters give their brothers when they say something kinda dumb.

"It's ok. I'm not scared." And off I went.

All the way up the hill to the bus stop at Maryland Avenue, I chatted with that voice in my head that advised against this rash display of competition from someone who had yet to produce any testosterone.

But as I turned my bike and aimed it downhill, that voice of reason was drowned out by the pounding of my heart, now thumping away at the insides of my ribcage.

I pushed off and started to coast. This wasn't so bad. I wasn't really going that fast. Instinctively, I pedaled some to get there sooner, looking with anticipation as our front porch came into view about a block or so away. I could see them all standing there…Fil, Susan holding Alice, and now my mom, wiping her hands on her apron.

In that same instant, I realized that my momentum had carried me much faster than I had ever been. Perhaps even three or four times faster. I could hear the chips of gravel kick out from under the tires as I whipped past the mailboxes.

In the next instant I thought of two things: first, that our driveway was dirt and gravel, not exactly the best for traction. The second thing was that the voice of reason had returned and was shouting at me, "Brake now! Brake now!"

Thing is, while I knew that's what I *should* do, I simply couldn't recall *how* to do it. *I can't stop*, I thought. *I can't remember how!*

Now I don't remember this part exactly, but my family tells me that I was shouting from the bike about 100 feet or so inbound. And it was what I was saying that likely saved my life.

"I can't stop! I can't remember how! I can't stop!"

Big brothers can sometimes be a real pain in the neck for little brothers; but in this case, Mr. Safety leapt off that front porch on an intercept course with me. His plan was to snatch me from the bike in mid-ride. All he had to do was beat me to the gum tree.

Susan dashed into the house to run cold water, while Mom ran to get ice. Alice cried.

My front tire hit first, then my head. Fil caught me midair as I bounced off the gum tree. And like a cornerback who has just snagged an interception, he turned and bolted into the house just as I blacked out.

The next thing I remember was lying on the couch and everyone standing around me, a painful, goose egg of a knot in the middle of my forehead covered by an ice pack the size of my skull. It only took a couple hours for the double black eyes to appear.

That evening, my dad made me get back on Blackie and ride around the yard for a few minutes to solidify my future braking skills.

Impressions are enduring. He talked with me patiently, encouraging me, asking me how many fingers he was holding up; you know, father-and-son stuff like that. I wear a helmet now when I ride. And as much as I'd like to show off to my grandkids, I learned my lesson: I make sure I'm not riding when I show off.

Of course, it probably didn't happen exactly like that, but that's how I remember it.

CHAPTER 3

· · · · · · · · · · · · · · · · · ·

My First Kiss

We looked at each other for a long time.

"Do you like me, Tommy?" Daisy Johnson half-whispered.

'Boy, do I!' I thought. She smiled knowingly. That was weird. Could she hear me think? We crouched together behind the azaleas underneath the old oak. Hide and seek was a lot more exciting in pairs.

"Isn't this fun?" her giggles seem to say.

There. She was doing it again, that "in my head" stuff.

"How much?" she whispered again.

"How much what?" I asked, keeping an eye out for my sister, who was "it."

"How much do you *like* me?"

"The moon!" I said, trying not to think about it too much.

What in the world did that mean? I thought quietly to myself. One can't be too careful around pretty girls with freckles and amazing hair that smelled like vanilla wafers.

Fortunately, my ability to think on my feet has improved over the years, but this was the best I could conjure up as a seven-year-old under the pressure of close proximity to Daisy Johnson.

"The moon?" she asked between snickers.

"Uh, yes. The moon." I repeated, less sure.

"That big, huh?"

"Yes. I mean, no. Bigger."

"Well, Tommy, my feelings for you are as big as Jupiter," she said, taking up the astronomical challenge.

"And my feelings for you are as big as the sun...AND the whole solar system together," I said, not to be out-liked.

She paused a moment. "I... like you as big as the Milky Way."

"That's big," I said, thinking that a Milky Way bar would taste pretty good right about now. "I like you as big as the whole universe," confident she couldn't like me bigger than that.

Daisy closed her eyes and furrowed her six-year-old brow, the giggles subsiding. I stared at her. Her eyelashes seemed almost unreal they were so long. Her green eyes rolled back and forth under their lids as she searched for someplace bigger than the universe. Her lips puckered ever so slightly, her reddish brown curls ruffled softly in the summer breeze.

As we sat cross-legged under the old oak tree on the warm, brown earth, the whole of the world became enormously quiet. I heard nothing but Daisy breathing. I saw nothing but Daisy sitting there. I felt as though time had stopped, the planet breathed in, and the world waited for Daisy to say something before it would dare breathe out again.

Anything.

It was in that still moment, with everything completely stopped, that I realized I wanted to kiss Daisy Johnson on the lips. I'd never felt like this before. I was terrified and overjoyed at the same time. Trouble was, I didn't know how to kiss a girl. And what if all this talk about 'liking me' was just that? Talk? My second-grade heart couldn't take the strain. Daisy Johnson was possibly the most perfect girl in the universe...

"I've got it!" Her face burst open in the biggest, ice-cream-sundae smile I'd ever seen. She took my face in her soft little hands, stared me in the eyes and leaned forward. I felt her breath on the end of my sunburned nose. Cotton candy. This must have been how Romeo felt about Juliet when they first kissed.

"Got. What?" I asked, barely above a whisper.

"How much do you like me, Tommy?"

How much? Hadn't I already told her? Didn't she know? Couldn't she read my mind? "My love for you could fill up an entire universe," I repeated, certain she couldn't top that.

"Love?" She wasn't nearly as shocked at hearing it as I was at saying it. My face must have registered my sincerity.

"Well," she said. Her eyes sparkled, obviously pleased. "My love for you is as big as God. Try topping that, Tommy Kimball."

I was stunned. That was a lot. Bigger than anyone or anything else in the universe, which He made, with Daisy in it.

She had me. I didn't know what to say or think or do. She started giggling.

"What? What's so funny?" I searched her face looking for the answer. No words.

"You. Your face is all red," she said, crinkling the freckles on her nose. "And you're breathing funny."

"Am not."

"Are too."

I gulped. My mouth was as dry as the dirt on my knees and my lips were crunchy like autumn leaves. How was I going to kiss her with crunchy lips?

"I, I, I... "

"E-I-E-I-O, country boy." Suddenly she pushed her face into mine. "You're in *love* with me, aren't you, Tommy Kimball?"

Can't breathe. I flopped back on my Thom McAnn high tops. Felt like the shoes were stuck in the back of my throat.

"You wanna kiss me, Tommy?" She giggled again. A roaring in my ears drowned out the sputtering from my throat.

"I, I, I... "

"Ok. You can if you want." She closed her eyes and puckered up.

For a long time I just stared at her beautiful, round face. I can still remember every detail: the galaxy of freckles across her pug, little nose; every strand of that reddish, brown hair cupping her face; the peach cheeks, the tiny earlobes, perfect eyelashes, and those lips. Oh dear, those lips...

And me? If I could stand—I was barely sitting up—I'm quite certain that my legs couldn't hold a note let alone my weight. If I could breathe—I'm quite sure I wasn't breathing at that particular moment—I was certain that I would have sucked in our whole back yard through my nostrils.

So, with fading consciousness and with what little power to reason that still tenaciously clung to my spiraling cerebral vortex, I decided to close my eyes, risk free-falling vertigo and kiss my beloved Daisy.

As our lips touched I felt as though gravity simply ceased to exist and I had swallowed my head. My eyes popped open involuntarily and I couldn't help noticing that there was someone else there with us. Not my mom. Not my dad. But the last person I wanted to see at that moment: my baby sister.

It was then that God decided to fill my first romantic experience with my furiously jealous little sister for what I can only believe was my own good.

To this day, I really don't know where Alice came from. I was certain she was in the attic of the house, hunting for Daisy and me. Then, in a microsecond, there she stood as though she simply materialized out of thin air in a hurricane of jealousy.

As suddenly as my first visit to "heaven" began, it was over. Like a blanket yanked off my quivering body, the cold reality of

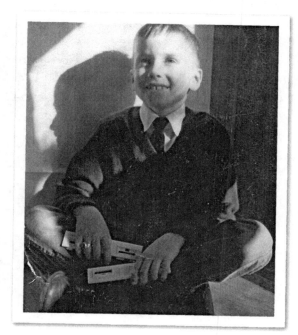

Who wouldn't want to kiss this handsome devil?

23

childhood rushed back into my world. Instantly, I was back on Earth, emotionally naked in front of my kid sister. I remember leaping to my feet while Daisy rolled over and burst into laughter.

Alice's usually sweet eyes narrowed into mere slits of chocolate ice. She looked from Daisy to me, and then from me to Daisy, as she ground her teeth and clenched her little fists.

"Alice, I can explain --" and before I could get the words out, something happened I couldn't explain: fire jetted from my sister's nostrils; out of her tiny throat erupted a shriek that stood up the hairs on the back of my neck. And suddenly, I was sent into orbit by a single punch to my solar plexus from my six-year-old little sister, who somehow found the strength of Rockette Balboa in the 15th round just before the bell.

To say that Alice knocked me out of this world is putting it rather mildly. Actually, she grounded me in reality again. She'd made her point. If I was going to explore that space between a sister and her best friend, I'd better navigate a bit more cautiously, and wear a cast-iron skillet around my waist.

Anyone who can remember his or her first smooch knows just how sensational and meteoric a first kiss really is. Just as memorable was the cold reality of sibling rivalry. Both last a lifetime.

Daisy moved away at the end of the summer to go to school on some distant planet in a galaxy, well, you know where.

Of course, as I linger on that first kiss, I must admit that maybe it didn't happen *exactly* like that, but that's how I remember it.

CHAPTER 4

· · · · · · · · · · · · · · · · · · ·

Mad Dogs & Paperboys

Every afternoon, McLhinney's old Chevy Suburban roared down Lyon Street to our gravel driveway. One of the McLhinney boys would throw out two bundles of newspapers, one of each kind—the Sun and the News—then they'd grind the gears and tear off up the street with our dog Missy trying to take down the old truck with her teeth.

"Dumb dog," Dad would mumble good-naturedly at Missy, prancing back to the house as if she'd really done something.

Like so many baby boomers, my first professional occupation was "paperboy." I delivered newspapers to about 50 customers in my rural neighborhood for $1.85 a week. Yep, you read that right: a buck eighty-five. Hey, for an 8-year-old boy in the mid-Sixties, that was a lot of cash.

I thought it was kind of cool, being a working man at such an early age. And the money, though meager by today's standards, was all mine. It made the time go faster. The sooner I was done, the more worthwhile it seemed.

Anyway, I'd drag the bundles onto the carport, roll the newspapers into thirds, and stuff them into my big, canvas newspaper bag. I'd sling the bag over my shoulder and hop onto my bike to ride the mile and a half route every afternoon after school. I did this for 20 years. Ok, maybe not that many, but it seemed that long. Being a newspaperman is hard on a fella.

I delivered the Baltimore Sun to most neighbors and the Baltimore News-American to a few. The Sun went into the pretty aluminum newspaper boxes while the News went into the cheesy, green plastic ones. The boxes were long, square tubes, usually fastened to the homeowner's mailbox at the end of their driveway.

I'd streak by from box to box on Blackie, my fender-less, 20", single-speed bike, slowing down just long enough to pop a paper into the box like I was dropping a mortar round into a launcher. It went like this: pedal like mad; coast; grab the paper; another pedal burst; coast again; reverse pedal to brake with my feet; anticipate the angle of approach and speed on target; prepare for release; load tube — thunk — and tear away to the next box.

I'm not sure what challenged me most: the seven-day workweek, the weather, the wasps, the customers or the dogs.

Weather-wise, it was a real drag when it rained or snowed or sleeted or hailed. On those days I had to walk, which took forever. We only had one car and my mom would rarely break away to take me. But, somehow I managed. I learned to work.

The wasps were a pain. They'd nest all the way in the back of the box. If I was too slow when I dropped the paper into the tube, a sting-fest would ensue. I learned to reconnoiter a suspicious box or one with a history of sting-age, and to adjust the velocity needed to make the drop.

Three boxes stacked together required a real balancing act. I would have to dismount, sneak up on the boxes from behind and carefully slide each paper until it was positioned just so, forty-nine percent of the paper sticking out of the box, perfectly balanced for easy owner retrieval.

Customers would complain sometimes if I missed a box or when the paper got wet in an afternoon storm (uh, what about the paperboy, hello?). Any-who, I did my best to keep them all dry, but I wasn't going to get stung for less than two bucks a week. Five maybe, but not two.

The dogs in the neighborhood were the bane of my paperboy career. Most of them I knew... and they knew me. Leash laws are relatively new in our culture. In those days, it seemed the dogs freely roamed the Heights in herds: snarling, drooling, foaming at the mouth, looking for their next journalistic meal...me.

Incidentally, during the last days of my early work in journalism, my big sister, Susan, who was 10 years older than I, was graduating from high school. She drove a green Volkswagen Beetle that my mom hated. Why did my mother hate a harmless little beetle, you ask?

Picture this: my mother and sister, motoring through the Blue Ridge Mountains, on their way back from checking out a college in Tennessee, with my mother gripping a handle on the dash, her wide-eyed face nearly pressed against the flat windshield, Susan whipping her VW Bug through the mountain passes.

Seems at some point during the trip with that front window just inches from her face, my mother, not considering the short distance and the length of her reach, broke her finger while vigorously pointing out some perceived impending danger to Susan. I'd have paid front row prices to be in the back seat.

Now anyone who has ever been admonished by their mama for pointing their finger can appreciate the peculiar irony of her busted pointer. They put it in a cast for several weeks but I swear she had it removed early. When she puttered around the house with that finger always pointing like a Frosty-snowman arm, it was distracting, and a little bit funny.

"Hey, Mom! What's the point?" Or, "Mom, how many brain cells is Alice using?" Mom would raise her hand and indicate "one" with that forever finger.

Anyway, where was I? Oh yes... so the summer I quit delivering papers was the week of the Newspaper Banquet when representatives of the two Baltimore media giants ventured out into the small towns and cities, to give the paperboys and their dads a big meal of spaghetti and meatballs to say thanks for spreading the news. (By the way, girls did not deliver papers in those days. They were too busy selling Girl Scout cookies. Honest.)

I had just finished my last run and was headed home past the Gordon place when one of the "ever-unattainably cool" Gordon kids invited me to come over and see their new swing set and monkey bars. Ironically, some of the coolest kids on my block had the meanest dogs in the universe. Wolfie (The Hellhound) was a mutt, but I think he fancied himself descended from the Baskervilles. I could believe that.

"Is Wolfie on his chain?" I asked, not trusting him nor the dog.

"Yes. Look."

I did. And there he was, snarling and barking in a far corner of the back yard by his doghouse. I parked my bike and leaned it against the monkey bars. Suddenly, Wolfie-hellhound stopped barking.

By the time I reached the top of the monkey bars, Wolfie was snapping on the ground below me. My knees went weak and I nearly soiled myself. I couldn't believe I'd been so gullible. The Mad Boys of Gordon laughed as I pleaded for my life. Finally, the eldest nutbag grabbed the hellhound's collar and promised to hold him tight until I got home, two blocks away.

After five minutes of convincing, I climbed down and kept my bike between them and me. I cried, stumbling down their drive and into the street. They followed me and stood in the front yard, taunting and teasing me all the way.

"Don't get on your bike and try to ride away fast, Tommy Kimball, or we'll let Wolfie snack on your skinny chicken legs for supper!" They always laughed at their own jokes.

About a half a block away, I made my move and jumped on my bike. Blackie was fast with me in her saddle. If I could make it to my yard, I knew I'd be safe. But true to their word, as soon as I did that, they cut the Mad Dog of Gordon loose and he gave chase.

As I approached the corner of John Smith and Lyon Street, I looked back over my shoulder; that mangy cur was gaining on me. I wasn't going to make it. I decided to stop and make a stand, so I slammed on my brakes and laid Blackie down in the gravel, skinning my knee in the process. The fresh blood etched a path down my dusty summer leg.

Tears streaking down my face, heart pounding my ribcage, jaw set, brow furrowed, I grabbed my bike and swung around and screamed, ready to smash my four-legged foe with a face full of spokes.

At that moment, as is true in a crisis, time seem to grind to a halt and everything that happened next occurred in slow motion.

Exploding into view like a scene from *The Love Bug*, my sister's green VW kicked up an angry cloud of dust and gravel and crunched to a stop between the hellhound and me.

She shouted to me through the open passenger window, "Get in the car!"

Susan, barely weighing a hundred pounds herself, grabbed an umbrella, leapt out, and lunged at Wolfie. The dust cloud, billowing around the car and engulfing the ensuing battle between sister and mutt, obscured my view as I strained to catch a glimpse of what was happening.

The dust settled and the sounds of whimpering dog and screaming children faded as she chased them back to the Gordon house. I swear she must've scared Wolfie so bad he became a cat. Never saw him again.

As for the Gordon Boys, I have no idea what my sister said or did to them. We never talked about it. Maybe they all became priests or something, I dunno. I was just grateful they never bothered me again.

Susan sure knew how to handle bullies. She taught me the value of facing down the dogs of life with fearless determination!

Ok, maybe it didn't happen exactly like that, but that's how I remember it.

CHAPTER 5

• • • • • • • • • • • • • • • • • •

The Cheez Whiz Mortar of '68

I could hardly wait.

It was 1968 and my first summer at scout camp. It would be an adventure of firsts: the first time I would spend so many days in a row away from home; the first time I would hike in the wilderness and camp under the stars; oh, and my first introduction to high explosives.

"Tenderfoot Tommy Kimball, Raven Patrol, Troop 967, Baltimore Area Council, BSA, reporting for duty as ordered, sir!" Yeah, that was me.

I spent a week packing my official Boy Scouts of America canvas rucksack with all my BSA gear: the obligatory BSA emblazoned scout knife; the official knife/fork/spoon combo in its pouch; my BSA compass; my extra summer uniform; swim trunks; underwear; BSA socks; flip-flops; towel, wash cloth, Ivory soap, toothbrush and toothpaste; first aid kit; rope; sewing kit; sleeping bag; and my favorite snack combo ... Nabisco Ritz Crackers and a can of Kraft Cheez Whiz. Yum.

Every stitch of clothing I wore or carried was labeled. Seriously. With my name. This was apparently customary in the years after World War II. Every kid, or nearly every kid (oh, I do hope I wasn't the only one) had their name embroidered on a roll of cloth tape six miles long that our moms would sew into our uniforms, underwear and socks. Everything. Why our little bottoms weren't tattooed as well is a mystery to me.

Fact is, in those days, we were required to wear complete uniforms: shirts, trousers, socks, boots, etc. Not like the more "casual" uniforms they issue the BSA today. We didn't have the option to wear jeans with a scout shirt. Ours were olive drab green cotton items, fashioned after the military uniforms of the day. So, dutifully equipped and bustling with excitement, off I went.

We all assembled on the north lawn of what was then the Havre de Grace Methodist Church. This was headquarters, HQ. Our troop met in the social hall every week. Parents dropped off their scouts and gear at the side entrance on Congress Avenue. Our bags were thrown into the back of a deuce-and-a-half and off we headed to Broad Creek Memorial Scout Camp on a warm and humid Saturday morning.

When we arrived at camp, there was a swarm of green-clad kids of all shapes and sizes. We buzzed out of the scoutmasters' cars—all massive gas-guzzlers and station wagons of the era—grabbed our backpacks, got our tent assignments, and settled in for the week.

As tenderfeet, the grunt duty of trekking to the quartermaster for supplies fell to us. It was work the older scouts didn't want to do, like collecting firewood and chasing after left-handed smoke-shifters. So they made us little guys do it to "build your character and discipline!" (Welcome to scout camp.)

On our way to the quartermaster just after lunch, my tent-mate, Jack Rothenberg, and I came to a fork in the path where we nearly bumped into a couple of older scouts from another troop bringing back their supplies.

"Don't take the Fox Trail to the quartermaster," said the Stout Scout.

"Yeah, it's off-limits," the taller kid added.

"But why? It's the short cut," asked Jack.

Stout Scout stuck his chubby face close to ours and said menacingly, "Yellow jackets." They walked off.

Yellow jackets are the meanest, most foul-tempered demon-wasps God created. So we took the longer, Cougar Trail to and from the quartermaster. When we were hiking back to camp, we noticed two kids were about to take the Wasp Path to Hell.

"Hey, guys! That path is off-limits!" I warned them. "There's a big yellow jackets' nest in there!"

"Says who?" the tough kid challenged.

Jack stepped in. "Says right on the sign, 'Off Limits'."

"I ain't scared of yellow jackets!" he said, mocking us as he turned onto Fox Trail.

"Yeah, how do you know, Tenderfoot?" the other sneered, "Have you seen it?"

"No, but these other kids said it was there." I tried to sound sure of myself.

"Listen to the crybaby scouts, Bobby, they're scared of yellow jackets!" They both were laughing as they took the road less safe. I could hear them still laughing as Jack and I picked up our basket and headed back the long way to camp.

A few moments passed and those laughing boy scouts were screaming like girl scouts. Later, after the running and shouting and stinging had died down, I overheard the scoutmasters say that one of the kids puffed up like a marshmallow blow fish and had to be sent to the hospital. Told you — demon-wasps.

Our troop was big, maybe 60 active kids and a dozen scoutmasters. Odd bunch, but a great group of guys, though I honestly don't remember most of them. Naturally, there were the stand-outs. There was Eagle Scout Mark Masters who could tie a timberhitch with his tongue. And there was Vincent Perelli who laughed maniacally while chasing and catching snakes with his bare hands.

Madness, I thought. Vinnie got bit a lot, but just didn't seem to care. He could be seen running through the campsite, day or night, in hot pursuit of one reptile or another, laughing and bleeding. Too bad he wasn't in the Garden of Eden. That old snake wouldn't have had a moment's rest to deceive anyone.

Broad Creek was a magnificent wilderness. Any adventure is possible in a place like that: hills to hike; rocks to climb; snakes to catch; canoes to paddle; caves to explore; a huge lake to sail and swim; and old canvas army tents and cots that smelled of smoky campfires, marshmallows, and ghost stories. All this while hundreds of others camped around you in a place where the Susquehanna Indians once hunted. Awesome.

So the first day wore on and we had made all our preparations, and then we enjoyed some time off in the late afternoon just to hang out in camp and talk and snack and stuff. As a boy scout, I was totally prepared.

The secret to a successful and delicious summer camp snack was, in my case, Cheez Whiz on Ritz Crackers. The Whiz comes in a pressurized can with a notched nozzle at the top that looks like a crown. When you press the applicator tip to one side, the processed cheese oozes out of the notched hole and you can make edible patterns on your crackers: stars, swirls, letters, secret codes, etc.

But it was more than just a tasty snack-tivity. With Cheez Whiz, you had friends, you had art, you had commerce! You see, I had figured out that not only could I make friends, I could sell my snack creations to the other kids in my scout troop. You know, for spending money at the commissary. Not a bad gig if it had gone according to plan.

Just as the sun was setting we had hot dogs and hamburgers with our patrol. Each patrol was bunked in a cluster of tents. Each cluster had a grill made from a 55-gallon drum which had been cut lengthwise and turned on its side with fencepost legs welded on the four corners to give it height. One or two leaders would cook over the wood fire we'd built in the grill.

After dinner, they broke out the marshmallows. The scout leaders would then leave us alone to our roasting, presumably to return to their tents for a cigar and a nightcap.

The dry wood snapped and crackled, sending sparks into the air. Pinecones, dropped onto the bed of hot coals, were particularly fun to watch sputter and sparkle. A real fireworks show.

But that was clearly not good enough for some of the more seasoned scouts. I'm thinking of one particular character from the other side of the tracks who was always looking for—and finding—trouble.

At some point this Scout-With-No-Name started tossing .22 caliber acorn blanks into the fire. We greenhorns didn't know what was happening at first, but we caught on fast. No longer safe to huddle around the fire, we backed away and just watched the show. No-Name soon ran out of ammunition and the excitement died down. We huddled around the fire again with our sticks and marshmallows.

Then, out of nowhere, something vaguely familiar plopped down into the middle of the red-hot coals. At first, it kicked up too much smoke for us to see what it was. Then, wide-eyed, my tent-mate Jack read the label aloud.

"Caution. Contents Under Pressure. Do Not Puncture or Expose to Excessive Heat."

He looked at me. "Hey, isn't that your Cheez Whiz?" he asked. I nodded.

Then the air cracked and we all jumped. The calm of the evening was disrupted, not because of the fire or anything in the fire, but rather by the shrieks of the nameless adolescent. He rolled around on the ground and cackled, pointing and mocking the startled looks on our innocent, little faces.

We all exchanged glances, our collective gaze finally coming to rest on the can. We were all frozen in place, uncertain of what to do next. It was like a scene from a scary movie.

I, however, had seen this film before. I was the first to move, turning away from the drum of pressurized doom, the can of cheese now hissing angrily from its resting place on the bed of red-hot coals. Then, in a flash, each boy spun away, dropped their marshmallow sticks into the fire and made the chaotic scramble for cover, running into each other, tripping over logs in the dark, fore-checked by the support lines running to each tent, diving behind trees, scampering from the impending explosion.

All of this frantic action was underscored by No-Name's incessant laughter and the hissing of the Cheez Whiz.

Then as suddenly as he started laughing, he stopped. This genius abruptly realized that he was alone. We were under cover and this knucklehead was left standing right next to the fire with the unexploded Cheez Whiz. We could see his face, lit by the flames. Eyes wide, he seemed almost hypnotized by what he saw in the fire.

Now I suppose he didn't really deserve any help, but hey, we were all trained Boy Scouts—you know, help your neighbor, "do a good deed" kind-of-stuff? A tiny voice cut through the darkness.

"RUN!" And he did. He had no sooner turned his back on the fire than the can exploded, sending a yellow mortar of steaming, molten cheese nearly straight up in the air.

Mind you, the sound wasn't all that loud, almost like that of a football kicked off a tee. But we all could see the glowing glob of goo escaping the hold of gravity and then succumbing to it-- on a perfect trajectory to intercept the kid who had thrown it into the fire.

All of us were watching as No-Name turned the corner by Scoutmaster Mentzer's tent and disappeared into the dark. My delicious snack hit the peak of the tent, then oozed down the canvas and plopped to the ground right at the feet of Mr. Mentzer, who had appeared out of nowhere. As he took in the scene, we had a perfect view of Mr. Mentzer clutching the collar of No-Name in one hand and his walking stick in the other.

So much for my cheesy snacks. As for No Name? He got a new nickname: Official Camp Dishwasher. He even got a merit badge for a job well done.

The other major fireside event I remember, just as vividly, was the Night of the Baked Potato.

It was tradition for each senior scout attending their last summer camp to take a couple of tenderfoot scouts out for an overnight survivor "type" stay under-the-stars. Our minimalist meal was a baking potato wrapped in foil and packed with some chunks of beef, carrots, onion and celery.

Out we would trek, and once we decided on a spot to make camp, we'd build a fire and shove our potatoes under the coals to cook while the "retiring" scout would tell us a story, imparting some great wisdom. I don't remember everything he said, only how it felt. (Turns out that's what wisdom is like.)

First, he told us about his adventures in camp over the years: about the kid who died after being bitten by water moccasins because he didn't look first when he jumped into the lake; about

Off to war or off to camp, the uniform makes the man.
Nothing drab about that!

the boy who was hit by lightning because he was out hiking instead of seeking shelter; and about the kid who got lost because he didn't have a hiking buddy (he was never found). He told us so many disaster stories that I'm convinced he either grew up to be a fireman, or he's now producing reality TV.

After scaring us into a sleepless night, he said, "Let's eat." Pulling the potatoes out of the coals and eating that "stew" by firelight was one of the most memorable meals of my childhood. In fact, he didn't say anything else until we were nearly asleep, staring up at the stars through the trees.

After a long time, in almost a whisper, he said, "From now on, and for the rest of your life, whenever you have a baked potato..." he paused, for effect, "...you will remember this night." And I have.

Life is still full of adventures. The firsts are fewer and farther between and there's nothing quite like remembering the best of them. To this today, I suddenly find myself sitting under that full moon, warmed by the fire that flickers in my memory, that same smoke bringing a tear to my eyes, misting over the whole scene from all those years ago. I'm perhaps the only grown man you'd ever meet who can be brought to tears by a baked potato.

Ok, so it maybe it didn't happen exactly like that, but that's how I remember it.

Boy Scout Troop 967 from Havre de Grace, Maryland, during the Summer of '68. The author is seated in the front row, fifth from the left, bare knees and looking like he's ready for a baked potato.

The Cheez Whiz Mortar of '68

PART 2

. . . .

An artist emerges...

MEADOWVALE
ELEMENTARY

ROOM   GRADE
17   4

SPRING 1967

Yes, two-tone turtlenecks were all the rage in the Sixties.

CHAPTER 6

· · · · · · · · · · · · · · · · · · ·

I Will Not Play the French Horn Like An Elephant

"Like golden flakes of heaven, are our children. Seeds of the Divine that sprout, grow, and reach skyward to their Maker, as if to say, 'Hold me, Daddy.'"

I wrote that line some time ago thinking of my grandchildren. I hardly think that's how Mr. Victor Franklin thought of us at band practice each afternoon in the fourth grade. His perspective seemed to be something more like this:

"Like rusty clunkers no one will drive, are my band students; bad fruit, sour and whiny beyond belief, growing sourer and whinier no matter how much they practice; when their so-called notes make their way through my hair-strewn ear canal, reaching my highly tuned and sensitive eardrums, the notes pause before they begin their assault; taunting me, as if to say, 'I'm going to drive you positively mad until your brain explodes inside your bald little head and oozes out onto your dinner plate,' and, by mistake, you eat it, thinking, 'This is very bad peach cobbler.'"

There's something very odd and very true about that run-on sentence. Mr. Franklin was not a happy man. But I'm convinced he did it to himself. I mean, he could have quit at any time and gotten a job playing in a piano bar in Baltimore.

Instead, Franklin spent weekdays torturing himself, trying to find that one musical pearl amongst all of those tone-deaf oysters who wanted to play the trumpet but were relegated to French horn or clarinet or — Lord have mercy — the triangle.

If the torture of an elementary school band in the country wasn't enough, Old Man Franklin also donned a robe every Sunday at the United Methodist Church in Havre de Grace and led his small choir, comprised of seven of the oldest singers in human history — Mrs. Wooten, Mrs. Banks, and Mrs. Rickert, their reluctant spouses, and my ever-present Great Aunt Vesta — in special music.

Every Sunday, for as long as anyone could remember, he faithfully led them through some very complicated offertory written a thousand years ago in fourteen parts but sung in half as many. God only knows what penance he was trying to work out.

In spite of all that, the non-musical circumstances which should have driven a truly talented man like Franklin nuts simply didn't. You'd have thought that Franklin--who clearly loved music--would have expressed at least some outward emotional frustration in response to the slaughter of all those innocent musical notes. He had ample opportunity; he simply never did.

Franklin was stoic. Stoic and very, very serious. Look up the word stoic. You'll see a photo of Franklin standing there wearing a black robe, a grim look on his face, leaning on a paintless 1964 Oldsmobile F85, cotton balls jammed in his ears and holding a plate of moldy peach cobbler.

Now to be sure, I knew none of this in the 4th grade when I decided to play an instrument. I loved music and I loved performing. And I was sweet on Kathy, who was one of those French horn players I just couldn't resist. Especially after band practice when our lips would be numb and puffed up from all that buzzing in the mouthpiece.

The idea of a bunch of kids with disparate backgrounds and a wide range of musical talent from "very little" to "desecration" was really appealing to me. It wasn't so much about being the best horn player who ever lived; I just really loved the idea of getting together with friends and making music.

If you've never played in a band, you might not understand. But we were part of something special, something bigger than ourselves, something social and exciting.

Franklin, who knew my family from church, auditioned me and we both discovered I had an ear for music. If I couldn't pitch and play on the little league field, at least I had the potential to play in pitch here. And I could sit next to Kathy in the band. On stage. Glorious thought.

So, I got my French horn, and brought it home from school. In those days, schools actually had instruments for the kids to use. They would find children who were willing to learn, loan out the instruments until they ran out of them, and there you had it: a school band.

A brass instrument is an amazing expression of art and craftsmanship. It's shiny and cool to the touch, beautiful to look at, delightful to hold in your hands; and when a talented musician swirls air through all of those pipes, that instrument assumes a mystical life.

But in the hands a fourth grader, it can become a weapon of musical destruction.

To a highly creative boy like me—who could be facing the rebels in the woods at the Battle of Bull Run in one moment, and fighting bandits in the old west town of Santa Fe in the next—handing me a French horn was tantamount to giving a toddler a wooden spoon and a pan and expecting him to sit quietly.

It didn't take me long to figure out that the French horn was a sound effects machine. It wasn't just a musical instrument that supported a melody by playing the bass line. Boring. In the right hands, a French horn can deliver melodious substance to a piece of music while evoking a deep, almost unconscious, emotional response from a listener. I didn't care.

A French horn, in my hands, can sound exactly like a charging, African elephant. Now *that* was an exciting discovery.

In a matter of hours I learned enough basic pachyderm dialect on my horn that I could simulate a whole conversation, in which a mother elephant explains to her calf the dangers of water holes in the Serengeti, and how stupid the wildebeest really are and why you shouldn't hang out with them.

My sister loved my new act and gave me the "thumbs up" when I said I was going to share it with the band the next day.

And so, after school on that Tuesday in November, as the band was warming up to practice the Christmas program music before Mr. Franklin arrived, I stood up next to Kathy and announced my performance piece, which I called: Mama Ellie Teaches Baby Tambo About Waterholes.

I began my story: "Mama Ellie was the oldest cow in the herd. She remembered everything. She knew where every water hole was and led the herd there safely every year. She sang as she walked."

I lifted my gorgeous French horn to my lips and began to sing in 'elephant.' "Blat!!! Bla-bla-BLA-bla-aaaaaaattt!!!"

"One day," I said, "Mama Ellie was telling Baby Tambo about the dangers of the water hole and how she had to fight off the lions to protect the herd."

I then reenacted the battle between the elephants and the lions. The elephants spoke through my shrieking horn with the lions growling between blasts on brass. They loved it. They laughed and started playing in my symphony with their own characters: wildebeests, birds, monkeys, hippos, rhinoceros and the like. All hooting and blaring and screeching and scratching and stomping to fight off the roaring lions, building to a crescendo of cheering as the lions were defeated! What a delightful cacophony! It was the best band practice ever!

"QUIET!" Mr. Franklin exploded, leaping through the doorway. He must've been running from some distance. Were we that loud? He glared at all of us. Only now did we notice that the door had been open during the entire African Adventure.

"Who started all this?" he asked, already knowing the answer, I think. I was the only one in the front of the room at his music stand.

"Tommy?"

"Yes, sir?"

"What were you doing?"

"I was telling a story."

"A story? All I could hear from the other side of the school was your French horn."

"I was playing my French horn like an elephant."

"An elephant?" He was incredulous.

"Yes sir. An African elephant."

Mr. Franklin had stopped panting. He righted himself, tugged on his little black sweater vest and now, fully composed again like the great conductor he was, crossed the room to me and said, "Tommy, please take your seat."

I couldn't speak. I looked at Kathy and she turned away from me. I was shunned. And I was in big trouble.

"Tommy, since you started all of this, I want you to write in your notebook a hundred times: 'I will not play the French horn like an elephant.'"

"Only a hundred times?" I mumbled, unwisely. The band collectively gasped in G-flat.

"All right. Two hundred times. And that will be due to me tomorrow *before* band practice."

Franklin shook his head, and I'm quite certain he mumbled, "Elephants."

Anyway, I wrote that sentence two hundred times. Might as well have been a million times. It pretty much destroyed any desire I had to play in a school band. I quit a few weeks later. Ultimately, though, it was a good thing. I got into the Christmas play instead.

That lesson taught me something about myself, about writing, and my creativity.

I learned that day that I'm not here to play the French horn like a French horn. I am here to play the French horn like an elephant. An African elephant, protecting and leading her herd while teaching her baby the secrets to good elephanting.

Of course, not all of us sing from the same sheet of musical memories, but that's how I remember it.

CHAPTER 7

$\bullet\bullet\bullet\bullet\bullet\bullet\bullet\bullet\bullet\bullet\bullet\bullet\bullet\bullet\bullet\bullet\bullet\bullet$

Chasing the Broadway Banana

I've spent thousands of hours as a performer onstage—
school, amateur and professional—during the last 40 years. I've
played everything from blood-sucking, suave creatures-of-the-
night to singing, patriotic men of power; from anxious, rich fools
to eager, classic heroes. It's likely you've never seen me perform,
and perhaps never will.

But as I recall those moments from all those plays and
musicals over the years intermingled with other pursuits, I must
tell you, there is nothing quite like performing in the theatre.

There you are on the stage, bathed in light, on a life-size
sculpture called a set. You're playing to a live audience, telling
and retelling that amazing story as if it were the first time you'd
thought of it, and that room full of willing partners is right there
with you — breathing, laughing, crying, gasping — in the darkness
just beyond the lights, sharing in your every foolishness.

Heady. The first time I realized the power of that spontaneity
and the joy of unified laughter was in the second grade.

Miss Hayden had decided that our class would provide a
menagerie of animals for the Christmas play. My mother had
this monkey suit that was probably made in the Victorian era.
I'm not kidding. I was surprised to discover as I grew older that
monkeys don't smell like moth balls.

Anyway, we didn't have much money so it had to do. It had no mask to cover my face like all the other kids'. It didn't even have ears. How was I supposed to hear? In fact, as I think about it, I'm quite certain that it wasn't a monkey costume at all, but rather a rabbit or a squirrel. It was a light tan color, like a worn-out towel. It had feet and it zipped up the back. I wore tiny white gloves and looked more like a brownish Daffy Duck than a dignified Curious George.

We made ears out of brown construction paper, which I really hated. I had to DRAW the lines on. The worst of it was the ersatz monkey suit had front pockets like my flannel pajamas. In fact, I wasn't sure that these weren't my PJs.

Good grief. If ever there was a Charlie Brown moment in my life, this was it. And my mother was Lucy. But I trusted my mom so when she held the football for me, I… uh, well, you know what happens.

Anyway, all of us in Miss Hayden's theatrical zoo were to wait backstage for our big moment to enter: a big group number when the whole herd of us would bound and frolic on stage. Then, while the third graders were gathering backstage getting ready for their number, I was to stay on stage and stall for time… as a monkey.

"What am I supposed to do?" I asked my teacher.

"Oh, I'm sure you'll think of something, Tommy! You're so creative!"

I was creative? Glad she thought so. I asked my Dad at breakfast what I should do.

He looked up from the paper and said, "What? Eat your banana."

So that was it. Pretty simple. Great direction. I would eat a banana until I was chased off the stage by the third graders. So I snagged the brightest yellow banana from the bunch on the kitchen table and stuffed it in my book bag along with my monkey costume, and off I went to school.

Now as I stood backstage clutching the banana-turned-prop while mulling over my stage debut, I gradually noticed that standing in front of me was Ellen Childers, a cute, curly-haired girl with legs up to her pigtails. Ellen could run all the way to the top of the giant sliding board without holding onto the sides. When she did that, I forgot everything else around.

Suddenly I was in that place again. The anxiety of my stage debut faded away. It would be all right. I was with Ellen now; everything would be okay. She was sixth-grade-tall, which, at Meadowvale, made her a perfect giraffe. All I knew was anyone who could hang from the monkey bars by her toes and draw circles in the dirt with her pigtails was okay in my book.

Miss Hayden screeched our cue and herded us onto the stage. This was it. Our time had come. I jammed the banana in my pocket. Off we galloped and hopped and bounded. I followed Ellen, as close as I could without looking obvious. I would follow her anywhere. I didn't care. Wherever she was, it was the Garden of Eden again and Noah had just dropped us off after the flood.

What I did not know was this: even though Ellen could perform amazing athletic feats on the playground, being on a stage in front of the entire school could push a girl giraffe beyond her limits. About the time we hit center stage, Ellen froze like, well, a giraffe caught in, uh, a spot light, which, as it turned out later, was being run by Ellen's big brother Chuckie, who had decided on his own that the entire show was about a giraffe. So with cruel precision, he trained the light right on my gal.

That's when it happened.

I noticed too late that she had stopped in the middle of the stage. To avoid running right into her, I tucked into a ball and rolled between her locked giraffe knees.

In the next few moments, I was definitely the "monkey in the works." Emerging downstage, I bowled down a few chipmunks and split a horse in two before landing on a foam purple porcupine named Cindy. I felt the banana squish in my pocket.

I jumped to my feet to try and continue my exit stage right only to have my feet yanked out from underneath me. What happened? Billy, playing the Stray Elephant, couldn't see where he was going because his elephant ears had flopped over his eyeholes; he had stepped and was now standing on my prehensile tail.

As I lay, a bit dazed, on the floor, my head at Ellen's feet, I realized that the audience was laughing... hysterically. I looked up. Ellen still stood there, statuesque, towering over me. I thought, "Why are they laughing at her?" Poor Ellen.

In the few moments I was lying there on my back, I realized that something must be terribly wrong with Ellen. I heard her whimpering. She swayed a little to her right. From where I was, I could see her upside-down face contort and twist. She looked like a weird puppet. Her eyes rolled back in her head and she started to drop...right on top of me.

Even though I was smallish and quick, I barely got out of the way before Ellen's head thunked onto the floor right next to me. The crowd roared. Applause! Instinctively, the Primate Hero in me leapt into action. I tried to pick her up. She was too much woman for me to move. I knew I had to get her off stage but could not budge her. More laughs. The harder I tried, the more laughter there was.

It seemed like an hour before Miss Hayden dashed out onto stage with the plump and stern woman with no name. She was known only as the School Nurse.

"Move, Tommy," Miss Hayden barked. I moved, right into the School Nurse. I bounced off her rather large presence only to find myself downstage center again, plunked cleanly in the spotlight where the frozen popsicle giraffe had once been. The audience was in stitches. I finally caught on that they were laughing because of... me.

The School Nurse scowled at me while she and Miss Hayden carried my Ellen away. All the other kids took that as their early cue and cleared the stage, leaving me to perform solo.

Ellen was a tough act to follow. I looked offstage hoping for some direction from my teacher who was hovering over Ellen, now awake, fanning her, holding her head between those long legs. I looked out at the kids. A titter of giggles rippled through the crowd. I didn't know what to do. So I started to walk off.

Some kid in the dark cried out, "Woo! Come back here!"

I froze, looking out into the cavernous blackness, then back at Miss Hayden. She gestured wildly, "Go on." I turned again to the audience. I looked up and walked around an imaginary banana tree. I then pretended to climb to the top and pluck a ripe banana.

It was then I stealthily pulled the smooshed banana from my pocket as I "climbed down" the tree. I then slowly began to peel that squishy banana. It was deathly silent as every eye was on me. No more laughs, just a collectively held breath, watching intently as I peeled back the brown and yellow skin to reveal – pudding!

I smelled the banana pudding. A giggle or two. I eyed that banana very carefully, examining it as if my life depended on it... mugging and grimacing at the mangled mess in my hand. More giggles. I slowly opened my mouth to take a bite and heard, I'm sure, a gasp from the house.

Now what happened next, I can't explain. Maybe it's how God amuses Himself, I don't know. But in that moment, *a clown was born.* I knew in an instant that to NOT take that bite meant my entire acting career came and went with Ellen Childers' fainting spell.

I froze and rolled my 7-year-old eyes toward the audience, then back again to the banana, becoming cross-eyed in the process as I focused on the very tip of the fruit. There, for everyone to see, was a bug. An ant probably, maybe a fly or cockroach or large bat, I dunno. There was *something* there and he was eating *my* banana!

Well, that just wouldn't do...so I opened wide and...chomp! I ate the banana, bug and all. The crowd "ew'd" and that's when I heard a thud backstage.

I looked over and there was Ellen clapping wildly, and passed out on the floor next to her was Miss Hayden, who had been watching me with the banana. Apparently Miss Hayden had an aversion, I think she called it, to eating bugs and fruit. It was too much, and I guess I was too convincing. The audience leapt to their feet!

Ah, the applause...

Ok, maybe it didn't happen exactly like that, but that's how I remember it.

CHAPTER 8

·····················

The Puppy of Christmas Past

I feel a little like Scrooge when I contemplate the ghosts of my Christmases past. I was definitely *not* filled with The Christmas Spirit the year my sister got a puppy, for example; all I got was, I dunno, something else that wasn't alive or that barked or pooped or peed on the floor.

I was so jealous.

Not that I would have been a very good pet owner at the time. You see, Alice was the gifted farmer-in-training, I wasn't. But that didn't matter. I was the older brother and well…you get the picture.

What comes to mind when I reminisce about those holidays? Sometimes greed overruns my tiny little man-brain, and I act like any self-respecting Scrooge: sometimes I remember what I didn't get for Christmas; or, more specifically, what my sister did get. Bah humbug, anyone?

Which reminds me, that year was the first time I was involved in a production of *A Christmas Carol*. It was to be the main attraction during the Christmas program at Meadowvale Elementary School that year.

I "auditioned" for Mrs. Bennington every chance I could to convince her to cast me as Scrooge. From Halloween to Thanksgiving, whether I was reading a story aloud for class, doing a report on the Taj Mahal, or reading the lunch menu, I put on my best Charles Dickens English accent to impress my teacher. To no avail.

I didn't get to play Scrooge on stage, but after petitioning my parents for a dog in vain, I was definitely "in character" that year.

You know the drill: the dog goes into a cardboard box in the neighbor's basement the night before, and is secretly smuggled in by "Santa" on Christmas morning before anyone goes into the living room.

When we were finally released to start unwrapping presents, I heard a scuffle from Alice's stuff and knew right away that she had trumped anything I had ever gotten (or was likely to get). At first I was stunned. I didn't know whether to cry or yelp. More aggravating than that was she didn't have a clue what was in her stocking. Not a clue. Oblivious.

I remember how deeply disappointed I felt, and how I hoped to miraculously find something just as amazing in my stocking. A covetous little bugger, I was. The closest thing to a live creature I got was an orange in the bottom of my stocking. It was sour. Like me that year.

I'm embarrassed to say that I wanted the dog to poop and pee on my sister's bed that Christmas night long ago; but now, I am deeply moved by how brilliantly perfect a gift it was for her.

She loved animals. Didn't matter what kind: cats, dogs, horses, squirrels, birds, cows... whatever. She talked about them, read about them, drew them, and sought them out. It seemed they sought her out, too. My kid sister was a Dr. Dolittle in the making. My folks knew that, and so she got the puppy.

What a lesson that was for me.

My sister was the happiest I've ever seen her (that is, until she married a dairy farmer). It was a perfect moment in time.

Which brings me back to that production of *A Christmas Carol* in the fourth grade. You might recall those famous words from the opening line of *Stave 1: Marley's Ghost* that Charles Dickens penned in the original: "Marley was dead: to begin with. There is no doubt whatever about that."

I know this book well now as, over the years, I have tread the boards of many a theatre in various productions of *A Christmas*

Carol. I've played Ebenezer Scrooge, Bob Cratchit, the Ghost of Christmas Yet To Come, and, of course, Jacob Marley.

In fact, it all began with old Marley whilst I was in that 1967 production by Mrs. Bennington's 4th-grade class. It was a performance of disastrous—nay, *catastrophic*—proportions. To this day, I'm not sure how what happened, happened, but it was clearly all my fault and consequently sealed my fate for the next 40-odd years.

What I can tell you is that most A Christmas Carol play versions are true to the book, no matter how condensed and abridged. The language, the dialogue, the metaphors, even the allegorical treatments--all express the exact feel and themes of the original. *A Christmas Carol* was so well written that it translates into nearly any form and still holds up. Remarkable. Genius.

I can also tell you that nine and ten year olds can utterly destroy the greatest literature in the world with no provocation whatsoever. Whether they spiral into chaos, confuse their audiences into stunned silence, or step blindly into the path of the Comic Train, these young pupa, lost between larva and adult stages, can drown out the classics with peals of laughter and frivolity where once there was great drama.

Here's how I destroyed *A Christmas Carol,* one of the most brilliant ghost stories ever written in the English language... and I did it, as Dickens wrote, 'all in one night.'

Johnny Hardwicke got the role of Scrooge, partly because he was the tallest kid in the class and partly because his dad was a county councilman. So I got cast in two other roles: Jacob Marley and the Ghost of Christmas Yet To Come.

On opening night (actually it was our only night) I, as Jacob Marley, was to slide through the opening of the wooden curtains on the gym stage, a hundred feet of the chains of this miserable life in tow, moaning menacingly.

When the time came, I struggled under the weight, dragging myself stage left to where Scrooge was to be waiting in his nightshirt, shivering in terror at my sudden appearance. But, much to my surprise, Ebenezer wasn't there. Fact was, Johnny was still backstage trying to fit into Scrooge's 19th century nightgown, which was about fourteen sizes too small.

I froze in the stage lights. The audience was breathless. "What's the skinny kid wrapped in swaddling chains going to do?" they thought. "What *am* I going to do," I thought, now panicked and breathlessly terrified myself.

So finally, I did what any spook would do: I backed up, precisely reversing the way I came in, kind of like rewinding a movie. Only this wasn't a movie, this was a play. Live. On stage.

The kids in the auditorium broke into hysterical laughter. They laughed again as I reappeared when Scrooge was finally there. They laughed even more when I delivered my lines — terribly dramatic, beautifully written lines — in a voice cracking under the pressure of stage fright and puberty.

What I didn't know in that moment of youthful shenanigans was that this audience of hysterical children gave me *my* perfect Christmas gift...a picture of my life Yet To Come: a life of laughter under the stage lights; a life of wry observation on the page; a life of peculiar perspective "unfettered by the chains of this life."

In that joyful moment I discovered that my life is about just that...giving people something to smile about, reminding them to love a lot and live life a little more fully. That discovery was a gift.

Giving the perfect gift is, in and of itself, the perfect gift, isn't it?

Of course, I can't be sure it happened exactly like that, but at the risk of encouraing an unwanted haunting, that's how I remember it.

The Puppy of Christmas Past plays dead for her owner
and her owner's jealous brother... the author.

PART 3

· · · · · · · · · · · · · · · · · · · ·

To cheek OR not to cheek...

The author... practicing "cheeky" poolside.

CHAPTER 9

· · · · · · · · · · · · · · · · · · ·

Some Things You Just Can't Fake

My troubles began when Brian Michael Monahan got to go to the bathroom *first* on the last day I ever washed the chalkboard in school. It not only impacted my entire elementary school career; it put me off yellow chalk for the rest of my life. Let me explain.

First I need to begin with a disclaimer: in no way do I condone ditching school. You would do well to encourage young students to seek perfect attendance records. In other words, be more like Forrest Gump than Ferris Bueller: stick to it with single-mindedness, rather than wasting your incredible intelligence on figuring out ways to beat the system.

On the other hand, I might as well be completely honest with you: if you *are* going to try and ditch Mrs. Hayden's 2nd grade class (like I did, once) by pretending to be sick, make sure you don't get caught faking it.

I honestly don't remember the names of most of the kids in that class, but Brian was different. I remember him not because he was, well, the size of a fifth-grader who had eaten a second-grader; I remember him because of what happened that day — and the look of complete and utter disbelief on his face when what happened, happened, because I couldn't wait.

Brian Michael Monahan, who stood a whole head taller and sat twice as wide as all the other kids in our class, ate and drank more than all of us combined. Naturally, this contributed to his enormous size, but also relegated him to the back row in our classroom. I'm guessing the teachers wanted him as far away from their apples as possible. Or maybe he obliterated their view of half the class when he sat in the front row. I guess it doesn't matter.

What *did* matter that day was that we simultaneously raised our hands to request a pass to the toilet; Mrs. Hayden let Brian go first. He had a Number Two Emergency, and I had only signaled a non-urgent "number one."

All the world's a stage, Shakespeare wrote, and all the boys and girls merely players. And so it was on that cool October afternoon in 1964 that—just minutes before the afternoon bell— Fate raised the curtain to play a cruel and hateful trick on me.

I was focused on the last assignment of the day, feverishly scratching out math problems on my Big Chief pad. I told myself it was for the extra credit, but in reality it was to keep my mind off my own tiny bladder. Oddly, the number one kept coming up.

Worse still, my seven-year-old bladder had actually reached maximum capacity long before I had the good sense to raise my hand. Now, 20 minutes and three pages of long division later, everyone had forgotten about Brian. I knew if I didn't relieve myself, I'd have bigger problems to solve.

When I raised my hand the second time for my now-urgent need, I was finally given permission to go. I bolted to the toilet door and swung it open.

And that's when we *all* remembered where Brian was.

Now, to understand the horror of it, let me describe the layout of the room. The rooms at Meadowvale Elementary, at least for the youngsters in first, second and third grade, came equipped with a work sink and counter space under the windows on the west wall. To get outside to recess, there was a door in the back on that wall, near Brian's seat.

On the east wall was the entrance to the room and some supply cabinets. In the back, more work tables and a bulletin board that ran the length of that wall. In the middle of the room, there were the desks and chairs for the students lined up on the floor tiles in four neat rows of five desks each.

Finally, to the north, in the front of the room, was the teacher's desk, a green chalk board that ran the entire width between the windows, and a small door to a water closet: a single-occupancy sink and toilet for the wee (no pun intended) people. This meant that every student in the class had a perfect view of the bathroom door, or, if the bathroom door was open, a perfect view of the inside of the bathroom.

Apparently, in his haste to deposit waste, Brian forgot to lock the door. So there he sat, perched on this miniature toilet in front of God and the whole class.

I wanted to walk away. I wanted to slam the door shut. But for one excruciating moment, I froze and stared in disbelief. Brian, with his teeth locked like dueling ivory sabers, hissed, "You are so dead, Tommy Kimball."

I slammed the door shut. Why I didn't just pee myself right then and there is a mystery to me. But I didn't. I turned and faced the class, trying desperately to erase the image of Brian from my mind.

Mrs. Hayden was trying valiantly to not laugh as giggles consumed her students. She assured me that Brian would be done in a moment, and would I like to do something to take my mind off myself?

Yes, please, I thought. *May I die now?* "Anything, Mrs. Hayden."

A moment later, she handed me the tools to clean the chalkboard for the next day's lessons: a great honor. Presumably she really hadn't thought this through.

I took the small bucket and wet sponge, trying to concentrate on keeping my bladder from bursting while waiting for Brian to come out so I could have my turn. I was so preoccupied, I wasn't aware that I was simply smearing the chalkboard with the sponge and not really cleaning it.

Mrs. Hayden gently brought this to my attention. "Tommy, you need to rinse the sponge between wipes." She sounded far away as I dunked the sponge.

The temperature was just right, the color perfect. And all that urgency? Well, it all came down to one thing, the "number one" thing that soaked my trousers and left a rather large puddle on the floor.

Peals and peals of hysterical laughter erupted from my classmates. At that exact moment Brian stepped out of the toilet, unnoticed by everyone but me.

Needless to say, I was mortified. And while I'm certain every child in there had done what I had done at least once in public since they had been potty trained, I doubt very much that any of them had peed themselves in front of the entire class. I got no sympathy.

I could think of nothing to do but try to clean up my humiliation and then walk home from school. I wasn't about to ride the bus home in my condition. Better late than mocked, I always say.

A lesson in honesty from the master: Big Sister Susan.

When I finally got home, it seems my mother called the school and spoke to Mrs. Hayden. She said nothing to me as I skulked into the bathroom, stripped down, and took a long hot bath. I barely ate dinner and went to bed way early.

I knew I couldn't face going to school the next day. I was desperate to stay home and give this whole thing time to blow over.

The next morning, brushing my teeth for the third time to avoid that long walk to the bus stop, I inadvertently discovered that rinsing my mouth out with water and spitting into the toilet sounded just like puking, or perhaps more accurately, projectile vomiting. In an instant, I knew I had my way out of this mess.

For the next several minutes I built up the tension and drama. I pretended to be on the pot, moaning. I could hear my mom and sister at the dining room table talking, just a few feet away, so I knew they could hear me.

Then I upped the ante and began moaning louder to cover the sound of filling a Dixie cup with water. I drank one and held the water in my cheeks. I then filled two cups and tiptoed back to the toilet. And in one loud moan, I spit the water into the bowl, simultaneously dumping both cups. The effect was glorious!

My mother was at the door. "Are you all right, Tommy?"

"Yes, mom. I just have a little upset stomach."

I prepped a second salvo.

"Are you sick?"

I had the perfect answer for her as I moaned and spit and dumped the water again. It sounded like I had hurled up a grapefruit-sized hairball.

Unfortunately, all my dramatic acting had masked the sound of my mother opening the bathroom door to look in on me. As I raised my head from the bowl, I caught a movement out of the corner of my eye and turned to see her standing in the doorway.

Dang.

She didn't say a word. I flushed the toilet, grabbed my coat and book bag, and left for school. There are some things you just can't fake.

Surprisingly, when I did get to school that morning, it seemed as if no one (except perhaps Brian) remembered exactly what had happened the horrifying afternoon before.

Actually, Brian was really cool about it. Seems my mishap made all the other kids forget about his moment of glory in front of the class. He behaved as if me peeing my pants was an act of courage or something. I let him believe that. I was just relieved that I wasn't going to get a thumping.

Depending on how good his memory was, if I saw Brian today I'd probably just say, "Ok, maybe it didn't happen exactly like that, but that's how I remember it."

Caught!

CHAPTER 10

· · · · · · · · · · · · · · · · · ·

Setting the Farm on Fire

Do you have any idea how many of us wouldn't still be here if it weren't for our mothers?

I should preface this by saying: I have a mother who would tell you that I'm very lucky to be here, and while she takes responsibility for having brought me into this world, I'm certain there are times when she must have had second thoughts.

Like the time I set McConnell's farm on fire on the Mother's Day weekend when I was nine (I'm banking on a statute of limitations). My buddy, Wilson, and I were playing with a box of strike-anywhere kitchen matches in the rock pile about a half-mile from home in the middle of a pasture.

It was particularly dry that year in Maryland. The spring grass was poking up through all the old dead grass which had been drying out all winter, just waiting for a couple of guys with a box of matches to come along. It burned pretty well, which we thought was pretty cool.

We'd light up some grass, then stomp it out. Then we'd move a few yards, tempt fate again, watch the grass burn, and stomp it out. Only, we did that one too many times. Frantic, we beat at the grass with our jackets until it was pretty much burning like, well, like a wild fire.

So what did we do? We ran... in the opposite direction of home. We ran for miles. No kidding. *Miles.* We ran like cowardly lions until we discovered an abandoned tree house in which to hide out until the, uh, heat was off.

The rickety platform was up about 20 feet in an old sycamore off Chapel Road near Webster Village. Of course, we had NO idea where we were really. We decided to stay there until the cops or the FBI or whomever we were running from came and hauled us away. But that's not what really frightened me.

It wasn't Dad, either. Surely he would understand. While I had not shown him by this stunt that I had mastered fire, at least I proved I could create a fire big enough to frighten a pride of lions and then roast a sufficient number of turkeys to feed our small town of Havre de Grace on Thanksgiving—should I live to see another.

My older brother would probably pull a Wally Cleaver (looked just like him, flattop and all) and say something clever like, "Gee, Tommy, why didn't you just set the whole town on fire?" My older sister, of course, would simply roll her eyes and pick the apple skins from her braces. My little sister would laugh. She laughed at everything I did, especially when I got into trouble.

The fear in my heart was really rooted in my mom. My nine-year-old brain was already conjuring up the scenario: she'd be crouching in the azaleas by the front porch, well after dark, wearing mother-camo which, in 1966, was a house dress and apron capable of blending into any environment, rendering a mother completely invisible to her wayward children.

And there she'd be, waiting for me. Then, just as my hand grabbed for the front door knob, she'd leap from the dark shadows; she'd thrust her pruning shears into my hand and order, "Cut your own switch, sonny boy, and it had better sing."

So that's why Wilson and I sat there in that splintery tree house, crying, yelling at each other, blaming the other guy for the fine mess we'd gotten ourselves into, until we were just too tired and hungry to do anything else but go home and face the music.

The bats were starting to make their evening meal runs by the time I got home, sweaty, sunburned, and smelling like I'd been at summer camp for a week roasting marshmallows. Surprisingly, my mother was not in the azaleas. She was in the kitchen warming up some meat loaf and green beans for me.

She spoke calmly, almost sweetly, like a lullaby, "Where have you been?"

Before I could answer, she added, "Did you have a good time?"

"Yes."

"Did you walk Wilson home first?"

Why would I do that? I thought. Then she waited for me to answer. I was terrified but I spoke deliberately, trying to remain calm but feeling as though I may crack at any moment.

"We were playing in the woods on the other side of McConnell's Haunted House. We decided to go for a hike and ended up near the Bodt's house on Chapel Road. We were playing in a tree house near there for a while and just lost track of time."

I told her small, infinitely unimportant details about the wildlife we spotted hanging out in a sycamore tree and how Wilson was hating school, and how we thought we saw a flying squirrel and chased it down until it got dark. Of course, everything I told her was one hundred percent true. I just omitted certain details, like the fire and the FBI and maybe going to prison for the rest of my life.

Although I was thrilled to be home and not see a squad car in the driveway, I was still a wreck. Somehow her complete and utter calm was more terrifying than the wrath I had expected. I knew she knew. She had to. How could she not? She was my *mother!*

She never said a word. It was killing me.

That was worse than the switch, more effective I think, because I've never forgotten that lesson. Who knows what great public buildings might have gone up in smoke if she'd handled it differently? Frankly, I've avoided kitchen matches ever since.

So, the next morning, Mom got the best Mother's Day ever: I recruited my dad's help to give her breakfast in bed and clean the house. I bribed my big brother to let me take the trash out for a week. I was the first one in the car, ready for church, I plucked flowers from the garden, scrounged up coins and begged my big sister to run me to the store for chocolates... you know, I gave Mom the works.

I confess it was painfully obvious to both of us that I was

buttering her up; but since I had always been the burr in her saddle, it was probably a nice break for her.

You know, as I reflect on growing up and making it all the way to adulthood, I marvel at how complex parenting really is. A lot of the situations I found myself in could have ended very badly indeed, had I not had a firm hand guiding me, and a pair of pruning sheers awaiting me in the azaleas when I got home.

My mother had every right to roast me for some of those shenanigans... like the time I took apart dad's binoculars and had no idea how to reassemble them. Or the time I climbed the old birch by the creek to pout, and got stuck in the top, 50 feet up in the air.

Or a hundred other times I wouldn't be here to tell about if it weren't for my mother's pruning shears.

Ok, so maybe there was smoke in my eyes and things didn't happen exactly like that, but that's how I remember it.

CHAPTER 11

• • • • • • • • • • • • • • • • • • •

Patty Punched Me So Hard I Peed

Patty Paddleford's little brother, Wilson, was one of my best friends until, late one spring, we set McConnell's farm on fire. Well, not the entire 100-acre farm. Probably less than an acre of it; but to me, it might as well have been the whole dang farm.

Of course, that's another story. (Chapter 10 for those of you skipping ahead.) You may want to lock up all the kitchen matches and aluminum foil after you've read it.

The truth is, after that Mother's Day weekend, Wilson and I didn't speak to each other for weeks. It was summer before I saw him again.

We hadn't spoken with each other because each of us blamed the other, which is exactly what we were doing again on this particular summer day.

"It was your fault for bringing the matches!" I said.

"It was your fault for wrapping the tips in foil," Wilson said.

"Yeah, well it was your fault for lighting the matches!" I sneered.

"Yeah, so, well, uh... " Wilson sputtered for the words. His face lit up. "Oh yeah! It was your fault for bringing the tape recorder and playing the theme song to *The Wild, Wild West* and yelling, 'Light the fuse, Artemus, light the fuse!'"

Ouch. He had me there.

But like any self-respecting eight-year-old, I wasn't about to be told off by a particularly short and obnoxious second grader, especially in my own front yard.

I was out front trying to do my chores—watering the plants and cleaning the huge concrete porch—as Wilson blamed me for the fire and for getting him grounded, all the while poking me with his fat, little, seven-year-old finger.

Like most folks, I can take a lot of abuse, especially when I know I can win if it ends up in a tussle. I told him to leave me alone and that I never wanted to see him again, which is what you did in third grade when little kids tried to push bigger kids around. I never really meant, never again in the history of the world.

What I really meant was that I wanted him to leave right then so I wouldn't get in trouble and so I could finish my Saturday chores and play in my tree fort after lunch.

But Wilson wouldn't back down. He kept at me, like his mother's Chihuahua, yelping at me with his problems. *Man, this kid is a hothead,* I remember thinking, my temper starting to rise. *He needs to cool off.* So, really without any further thought, I turned the hose on Wilson and soaked him to the skin.

Naturally, he was surprised. But that quickly turned into furious sobbing. I watched him run up the street, leaving a trail of water behind. Yeah, going home to tell his mama what Tommy did to him. Big deal. My folks didn't really pay much attention to the Paddlefords.

They were polite whenever Mrs. P. called and reported that Wilson said I did this or that. Everyone knew that was how Wilson tried to cover for his own ornery streak. Wilson was just a crybaby and a tattletale; he did it to everyone. Maybe it was because he was the youngest and shortest in his rough and tumble family. I don't think so. He wasn't a bad egg, as my dad would say, just a bit scrambled.

I glanced up the street again as Wilson waddled around the corner on Maryland Avenue and disappeared out of sight. I went back to cleaning the porch. He'd be home any minute and the phone would ring.

But it didn't ring. I stopped squirting the porch and listened for anything from the house. Nothing. I walked around to the back yard. There was my sister on the swing, my mom hanging the wet laundry on the clothesline to dry, and my dad transplanting another azalea bush. Hmmm...

Then I heard it. At first I thought it was the sound of screeching tires on the asphalt, about a block away, near the mailboxes. *There it is again. No. That isn't the sound of rubber burning on the street; it's screaming. What are they yelling?* I moved back to the front yard to get a better view up the street. My blood ran as cold as the water dribbling from the hose into the lawn where I stood.

It was Patricia Irene Paddleford. And the screeching was her version of my name: "TOOOOMMMYYYY! TOMMY KIMBALL!!!"

About the time my thoughts made contact with my feet, our eyes met. My feet then belligerently ignored the internal screams from my brain to run. I was frozen.

Maybe she didn't really see me. I tried tricking myself into thinking this wasn't really happening, and turned back to my chores. It didn't work. Patty rolled in like a tank off the street, down the driveway, across the yard, and right up to me...nose-to-nose. She was so close, I could smell the cigarette smoke on her from her dad's unfiltered Camels.

You need to understand that Wilson's big sister, Patricia Irene Paddleford (everyone called her Pip for short), was more than just a neighborhood bully. She was THE neighborhood bully: the meanest, toughest kid in the Heights. Everyone was terrified of her, including, I suspect, her parents. She was absolutely fearless. It was great to have her as an ally but suicide to cross her. And while she was only a year older than I, she was stockier by at least 20 pounds of 100 percent lean beef.

Then she spoke. Her voice was very quiet and punctuated. I could barely hear her above the hissing sound coming from the hose.

"Did you squirt Wilson?"

Since my brain wasn't communicating well with my feet, it now tried to engage my mouth and respond with something that would essentially save its life. But every synapse in my body was seemingly impaired, which meant I was moving too slowly for Patty.

"I'm not going to ask you again, Tommy: DID. YOU. SQUIRT. WILSON."

Now maybe it's genetics or maybe I'm just a glutton for punishment. Either way, I can't really explain why I said what I said next. Seems my brain works at lightning speed when it recognizes an opportunity for humor.

"Yes. Wilson is a squirt."

The moment the words left my mouth, my brain screamed in terror, betrayed by that wicked little tongue which was now sticking out in Patty's face. Half of me cheered, the other half stood outside of myself in utter horror and disbelief at what I had just said to Pip. But instead of that terror registering on my face, I flashed a Cheshire grin...the kind that either saves or destroys. You can guess what happened.

In the very next instant, the wind rushed out of both lungs before I felt the pain of Patty's punch. Pow. I was on the ground, gasping for air.

Patty was now wearing that Cheshire grin and standing over me, watching me writhe and struggle to hang on to life.

"That's for squirting Wilson. Don't do it again."

She watched me moaning in the front yard for a few more moments to ensure that I was sufficiently punished before she turned to leave.

Now I'm not one to look for trouble, but if I'm in it, I'm not going down without a fight—especially when bullied. I snatched up the garden hose and let loose a volley of cold water on Patty.

The stream hit her square between the shoulders first. She wheeled around so fast and was so shocked by my counter attack that she lost her footing in the wet grass and started to go down. Then I violated the code of squirting and aimed for her gaping mouth.

I've always been somewhat of an expert marksman, and this was no exception. I filled her mouth and face with water. She fell on her backside in the mud, sputtering and coughing in disbelief and, of course, madder than a hornet. That's when I made a run for the tree fort. If I could make it there, I knew she couldn't follow.

I darted past my sister and mother as they were going into the basement. They didn't see me. As I rocketed through the backyard, I caught a glimpse of Dad on the far side of the yard, his head in a hole, all his attention on those azaleas. No rescue from any family members. I reached the tree fort in the woods in our back-back yard.

I was halfway up the rope ladder when I heard her calling me, ever so sweetly.

"Hi, Tommy! Thanks for inviting me over to see your tree fort. I'd love to come up and see it."

Wicked little vixen! She was pretending to be my friend, but I knew better. She was going to pummel me.

I could hear her footsteps now as I reached the platform and turned. Panicked, I realized she would make it to the ladder before I could pull it up.

Then suddenly our dog, Missy, thinking that this was all some sort of game, checked Patty at the knees. Patty went down just as she grabbed for the ladder. She missed.

I yanked up the ladder; I was safe. She lay on the ground beneath the fort for a good minute or two, catching her breath, composing herself. Missy kept trying to play with her. Patty growled. Missy backed off and went to her doghouse.

Patty then growled at me, "I'm gonna kill you when I get up there."

For the next hour she circled the tree fort, taunting me. It reminded me of *Peter and the Wolf*.

And it was lunchtime.

I tried reasoning with her, to no avail. I pleaded for mercy. I begged forgiveness. I threw empty threats at her. I cried. I yelled. I spit. She seemed to relish the power she had over me. And I was just feeding it.

What happened next may seem like the act of a desperate boy and a coward, but it was my last resort. I felt, after all that had happened, I had to do something. So...

I peed on Patty.

She never saw it coming. She had two brothers, one older, one younger, and neither of them would ever cross her. They had tried and she had beaten them to a pulp. She outweighed me. She was a Russian Cossack and I was a budding, young, sensitive artist.

I know it was wrong. I knew it was wrong then. But I believed I had no other choice. It sure took the fire out of her fight; it rained on her parade, so to speak.

Somehow, in that simple, disgusting act, she knew I would resort to anything to protect myself, and that I wasn't worth the fight anymore. And I imagine that she didn't smell very nice either.

She walked away from me without another word. She stopped only long enough to hose herself down in the front yard before heading home.

I watched her from the tree fort until she vanished from sight. I waited for another half hour before coming down and making a wild dash to the house just in time for lunch.

As I washed up and sat down at the table, my mother looked at me, then outside, then back at me.

"Didn't I hear you playing with someone in the back yard?"

"Pip."

"You think she wants to have lunch with us?"

"Nah, I don't think so. She left. She was kinda P.O.'ed that I squirted her and Wilson."

Mom wasn't really listening, but my sister Alice sure was. She looked at me from across the table with a look that said, "What happened?"

I shot back a glance that said, "Tell you later."

We had beanie-weenies for lunch that day. How appropriate.

Looking back, while I can see the humor in that episode, I'm ashamed of having resorted to such crude behavior. In the long run, I've learned that being P.O.'ed doesn't necessarily warrant being peed on. After all, Patty was just defending her kid brother. I would have done the same, I suppose.

I am certain that God has a way of sorting these things out;

ironically, I ended up with kidney stones.

I look at that as a kind of penance for peeing on Pip that day. (Sorry, Patty.) And I've never intentionally (or unintentionally) peed on anyone else, before or since.

Of course, if you ask her, maybe it didn't happen exactly like that, but that's how I remember it.

CHAPTER 12

· · · · · · · · · · · · · · · · · ·

Mother's Flying Frying Pan

Autumn in Maryland is an amazing season of transformation. Millions of trees bleeding all sorts of colors and so much excitement—a new school year, new things to learn, the anticipation of turning another year older. And when I was growing up in the 1960s, it seemed like most of those trees were growing in my neighborhood. It didn't hurt that we lived out of town next to the farm, either.

Coming home from school in the crisp air was always a treat. It was that time of year when it was cool enough to keep most of the windows in the house closed, except when my mom was baking. Then she'd open the windows in the kitchen, allowing the aroma of her German-baking heritage to waft through the neighborhood.

And like a lighthouse beacon to my nose, when I stepped off the school bus on those afternoons in October, I could always tell from two blocks away when mom had freshly baked bread waiting for me on the table. Unfortunately, so could all the other kids.

"Hey, Tommy, can I come over and play?" Johnny Wenn said, trying to act casual.

"No." He only liked me for my mother's bread. His mom

bought Wonder bread. It was a wonder, to be sure.

"Aw, c'mon! I'll give you my Hostess cupcakes at lunch tomorrow. No, cupcakes AND a dime for an ice cream sandwich." Now that *was* tempting. I didn't get dessert from the school cafeteria very often. Only cookies from home. *Hmmm...*

"Please? I'll let you play with my Johnny Unitas helmet." Johnny was persistent, I'll give him that.

"Ok, but not right now. Come over in about half an hour."

Johnny let out a war whoop and dove head first over the hedge into his front yard. "Good grief, Johnny! It's only bread!" He didn't hear me. He was already inside.

Only bread? Who was I kidding? My attention was now solely focused on the mission at hand: getting home to the hot, buttery, warm bread slathered with jelly before my kid sister, Alice, did. She was already a half a block ahead of me.

"T-Alice!" I tried to sound calm and confident. "Wait up!" I called her T-Alice (we all did) because when I was learning to spell, she wanted to be like her big brother (they all did) and spell, too. Mom would ask me to spell my name, which I did. "T-O-M. Tom." "Very good," she'd say. And Alice, who ALWAYS wanted to do EVERYTHING I did, would say, "I can spell, too, Mommy. Watch. T-Alice." And they'd all laugh and say how cute she was and it didn't matter anymore how well I could spell.

So when I asked her to "wait up" it was then that Alice—without turning around to look or even respond—Alice, my sister, my best friend, my confidant, my colleague in a thousand battles, my partner in childhood, my dependable, loving sibling who stood up for me and flattered me unceasingly, who worshipped me even though she knew I was mortal; Alice, my very own flesh and blood—bolted for the house.

Now, we Kimballs were always kinda skinny and not so tall. All legs. If you didn't learn to run fast, you'd find yourself with more bruises than the kids who were slower but not nearly as fun to beat up. I taught my sis to bolt like that if she ever found herself in a situation where she thought things might go badly, and she learned well. Did I mention that we were all born with long legs?

So she managed to slip through the back door into the kitchen and lock it before I could get there. That meant I needed to go in through the front door.

Now I need to stop here for a minute and tell you that my mother cleaned the windows once a year in the fall. In those days, we used all sorts of deadly, caustic chemicals to clean windows, strip lead paint off the walls, or just to mix together and see what happened. Chemicals which, if you bought them today like we did then, you'd end up on a Homeland Security watch list.

Mom had washed the windows that afternoon as well. But what I didn't know was, at the very moment I crossed the threshold and dashed into the house, mom had just burned dinner and the peach cobbler for dessert. I had entered the target zone.

Here's what happened: when Alice came flying in the back door, Mother thought something was wrong and was alarmed. Though it only distracted mom a moment, it was long enough for her to shift the focus of her wrath from the burning meal to, well, me.

When I came in the front door a moment later I was already salivating with the thought of scarfing down the heavenly gooeyness of freshly baked bread. I took a deep breath in anticipation of filling my young lungs with the indescribably delicious aroma.

Instead, in one breath, my nasal passages were singed with the smoke from flaming meatloaf, blazing peach cobbler, and charred green beans, mingled with the stench of ammonia from the window cleaning. This must be what Hell smells like.

Quite naturally, my olfaction being very keen, I felt obligated to comment on the experience. Alice frantically motioned from the bottom of the stairs in the corner of the dining room to stop me from saying anything to provoke my mother.

But being the older brother I ignored her warnings and said to my volcanic mother what she always said to me, "So what have *you* been doing all day?"

To me, that was a mostly innocent question with humorous intent. I was just trying to lighten the mood. But to mom, it was an accusation. It was insolence. It was felony.

In that moment, my dear mother, the woman from whose womb I sprang forth ten January's before, picked up the nearest object — in this case a frying pan — raised it above her head like a discus, turned, and in one Olympic movement hurled it across the kitchen. It cleared the doorway into the dining room in a flash and was on course to remove my head from my shoulders when gravity took over.

Fortunately for me, the oak dining room table was between us, and as I ducked under it the pan crash-landed on the table and shattered the glass peppershaker. A cloud of black pepper mingled with all the other smells and hung there, above the table, like a bad omen. I stood up.

I could see my mother standing in the kitchen through the pepper haze. My sister was frozen on the stairs. She'd seen the whole thing coming. I think we were all shocked. At least, I was. Quite unexpectedly, I sneezed. Four times. Or was it six? On the dinner plates.

Before you could say, "Gesundheit," Mother pointed to the front door and said in a low voice, choking back her rage, and perhaps a sneeze as well, or maybe both, "Wait for your father to come home — outside."

So I did.

I sat there for about 14 hours, it seemed, before I saw Johnny Wenn *running* down the street, obviously eager and anticipating his treat, Johnny U helmet bobbing on his pointy head.

He rounded the end of our driveway, slid to a stop in the gravel, and saw me sitting on the porch, book bag still in hand... but no bread.

We didn't have to talk. He knew. Slowly he removed the helmet. His shoulders slumped as he turned and wandered home. I can't be sure, but he may have been crying.

When Mr. Carson dropped my father off from work a few hours later, Dad didn't say anything either. Somehow he knew, too. He dropped down on the porch next to me. We sat there quietly for some time before he said, "Boy, you got somethin' to tell me?"

So I told him the story I've just told you.

He looked at me, or rather, through me. "Really?" he seemed to say. I knew that look. Quizzical, yet secretly amused.

Then my father sighed, picked up a crunchy brown oak leaf, and while he twirled it between his fingers he told me something about himself I've never forgotten.

"When I was about five years old, I crawled into one of those long, narrow drain culverts under a street in town near the lighthouse," he said. "It's a curly pipe about 18 inches in diameter. A little bigger than the one under the gravel at the end of our driveway."

I nodded my head and tried to imagine my father squeezing into that pipe. Hard to think of him as a kid.

"Well, I got stuck. For hours," he said, watching the leaf spin. "No one could hear me calling for help. Probably would've been days after I died and things started to really stink before they found me."

And I thought things smelled bad here.

"But like so many dumb things I've done in my life, I managed to wiggle my way out of that one," he said. "A scary lesson, but I was wiser for it."

He crunched up the leaf, letting the bits fall to the ground at his feet.

"Can't wiggle your way outta this one, son. Whatever you've done, you gotta own up to it and apologize. Let things fall where they may." And with that he got up and started into the house.

He stopped and turned to me as he opened the door. He closed his eyes and drew the air in through his nose. He breathed deeply a few times. It was an amazing feat of superhuman prowess.

"Mmmm…is that homemade bread I smell?" he said, loudly enough for my mother to hear his soothing voice cut through the foul air.

He held the door and waited. I stood up. He waved me in with his aluminum lunch pail. I took a deep breath, too, and held it as long as I could.

It actually felt good to apologize. I got an extra thick slab of hot bread smothered with fresh, melted butter and elderberry jelly as a bonus. I was a new man. Autumn was indeed a season of transformation.

As I reflect on that day, I realize now that we got homemade bread because mom loved us. And dad loved mom for better or worse. And me? I learned that love isn't about getting what you want. It's about giving your loved ones what they need.

Of course, it may not have happened exactly like that, but that's how I remember it.

PART 4

······················

Homeward Bound...

Hand-in-hand, the author and his little sister, Alice, exploring the possibilities.

CHAPTER 13

• • • • • • • • • • • • • • • •

Puddles of Infinite Possibilities

It rained a lot when I was growing up. More than it does now. Must've been a period of global saturation or something.

I have always loved rainy days. Even after I learned how rain happened, I was—pardon the pun—mystified by the magic of water falling from the sky. It was the most amazing thing to me.

The raindrops in the Maryland showers of my childhood were warm and lazy. It seemed the humidity slowly decided to take the plunge and become precipitation. It was magical, life-giving, and like the budding trees and flowers and plants, I thirsted for rainy days to balance my moments in the sun.

Most kids just wanted to stay home, drink hot chocolate, and sleepily watch cartoons on rainy days. But I became more acutely aware. I would see details I simply didn't notice in the sunshine. Those rains sparked my imagination, heightened my senses and drove me to places of sheer adventure. I could get lost chasing imaginary wildlife in the rain.

I loved what the rain did. It made things grow. It made things wet. It made colors brighter. It watered love and friendship. It washed away the dirt and made things fresh and new again. It gave pause to hope for a brighter, even more colorful day tomorrow. It made raincoats and umbrellas and boots necessary.

Each weekday, my sister and I had to walk a couple of blocks to catch our school bus. Our street was dirt and gravel in those days. In the spring, when it started to turn warm, I'd wear shorts to school underneath my big yellow raincoat. You know the kind of slicker I mean with the big, brass clasps? I also had a pair of black, rubber boots, with four of the same type of metal buckles. The boots were meant to go over my shoes and they were meant for puddles.

With my book bag in one hand and my Lone Ranger lunch pail in the other, I'd trundle out the back door. The moment I'd clear the carport, the steady chatter of rain would sprinkle my hood. It was music, a score written just for me. The sound still resonates with me. And I remember still the smell of wet soil and trees mixed with the distinctive odor of wet, vulcanized rubber.

I felt like I could weather anything in that big raincoat and boots. I was Jacque Cousteau or Robinson Crusoe or John Glenn.

The rainwater formed streams on either side of the street. Those streams would race downhill to our house at the end of the street, where it would flood our front lawn, much to my father's consternation. But it was a puddle wonderland.

My mother's voice still echoes in my head, "Stay out of the puddles!" I couldn't really. I would go out of my way to trounce through the puddles and streams of water. Holding hands and giggling in sheer delight, my sister Alice and I stomped through the rain-soaked carpet of mud while it was still showering. The edge of the puddles, where the grass met the dirt, was stickier than in the middle of the puddle. Oddly, there in the middle, the dirt seemed almost clean. To us, it was better than the beach.

I remember my Mom sitting on the carport snapping beans or peeling potatoes and watching us play in the puddles. I sometimes wish she would've taken off her house shoes just once and splashed with us. I think she would have liked it.

In my head the rain always "plays" that great Sixties hit by the Chiffons, *One Fine Day*. Then I imagine what might have happened if Mom would have stopped just long enough to listen and hear the music we heard splashing in those puddles.

The rainwater would play the pools of water like mallets on

a xylophone. The plinks in the puddles mixed with the slapple of the drops tapping the leaves, and together they drummed out a tune a kid couldn't help dancing to. It would build to a crescendo — Mother Nature's song.

My sister and I would swing round and round, the water streaming down our happy faces, contagiously tapping our little bare feet in the puddles, adding to the frenzy. "Hey, mom! Listen to that! Can you hear it?" Then we'd start singing, making up a rain song to celebrate the puddles!

In my mind's eye, Mom would suddenly kick off her shoes, throw her arms in the air, step off the carport and dance and sing with us. She'd sing those lyrics, "One fine day, we'll meet once more, and then you'll want the love you threw away before, one fine day, you're gonna want me for your girl!"

My sis would pipe up and sing the, "Shoo-bee-doo-bee-doo-bee-doo-bee-wop-wop!" part over and over.

Next thing, Mrs. Campanelli's sons — my baseball buddies, Mrs. Mingle and her two boys, Mrs. Baldwin with her girls, the Wenns, and the Nasticks — all would run out into their driveways, singing and dancing in the rain, joining us in a spectacular Gene Kelly moment...

The reverie and the music stop, and I realize that we all dance to a different rainsong.

Children do all they can to get wet. It's very sad that as we grow older we do all we can to stay dry. Adults put on boots to keep the water out. Children put on their boots and find clever ways to let the water rush in.

I'm certain that my sister and I became the best of friends, in part, because of rain. It was one of those things we enjoyed together, forever binding us in a way that's difficult to explain to anyone who doesn't have a brother or sister with whom they were close.

I know it doesn't happen with everyone, but it did with Alice and me. We were earth-bound Puddle Jumpers, the Giggle Gang, Jungle Explorers. Rain always brought that out in us.

I think God designed puddles for walking and splashing. I think He likes it when water gathers people together in "puddled" fellowship…particularly smaller, countrified puddles where dirt and bare feet meet to make mud.

And as the rain pelts the windows outside now, I have to be honest with you. Maybe it wasn't *exactly* like that, but that's how I remember it.

Dancin' with Mother.

CHAPTER 14

• • • • • • • • • • • • • • • • • • • •

Lost in Lancaster

To me, starting school was like being reborn, becoming a new person, in a way, or preparing for a role. And for a skinny kid from the country, who lifted his weight when moving a bag of sugar from shelf to cart, learning how to perform on the odd and demanding social stage of primary school was a huge undertaking. I needed all the help I could get. It started with the clothes.

My mother wanted to be sure that I had everything I needed for school, that I was prepared. Each school year, the schools handed lists to parents: mimeographed, smelling blueberry sweet and barely legible.

In the late summer months, early September, we'd drive the 90 minutes north to Lancaster, Pennsylvania, to buy clothing, which, in those days, was tax-free in the Keystone State. Some of the largest department stores in the Mid-Atlantic States were just over the border in PA.

All the country roads my father would take from Havre de Grace to Lancaster were dotted with road-side stands every few miles: pumpkins, enormous ears of sweet corn, apple cider, and bushels of luscious, freshly-picked apples that cracked when you bit them; all at pennies on the dollar.

I could always count on at least one horse-drawn, black Amish carriage to slow traffic to a crawl, and, of course, there was that all-important, one-of-the-firsts, modern, indoor shopping center in Lancaster called Park City Mall. (Yeah, I know, huh? A mall. Weird to think that at one time there were no shopping malls anywhere. Perish the thought. We survived it.)

Anyway, the year I started first grade, 1963, we went to this one particular department store the size of Delaware. No kidding. It was ginormous. They had golf carts running from department to department. The front of the store was so far from the back that they each had their own weather patterns. So it's not hard to imagine how easy it was for me to get lost.

Preparing for school meant trying on clothes to see what size we were, then buying new underwear, socks, a winter coat, gloves, and boots. It was kind of like choosing a costume. Don't get the wrong idea here; we're not talking about a huge, new wardrobe. Most of what I needed I got from my cousin, Sam, who lived in Havre de Grace. Not that it mattered much to me then because most kids in those days wore hand-me-downs from their rich, in-town cousins. I was no exception.

In a way, how I dressed in those days was a direct reflection on my Aunt Ruth's taste in clothes for Sam. She was also my biggest fan when it came to theatre, too. I played a lot of comedies when I was younger. Perhaps it was in part because I was funny; I think it was mostly because I *looked* funny in those hand-me-downs.

Regardless, Aunt Ruth had the best, most contagious laughter ever. I made sure she was invited to every show I ever did in school. I got the biggest laughs. I learned to whistle in her Sunday school class, too, right in the middle of Noah and the flood. You'd think that would have gotten me trouble. But it didn't. All I had to do was make her laugh and she'd cackle, we'd all crack up, and she'd say between chortles, "Oh, Tommy, I'm going to tell your mother." And then I would do my best Bill Cosby impersonation of Noah and the Ark and the elephant and she'd start laughing again and forget to tell my mom anything except how funny I was.

Back in the Lancaster Mall, Mom and my two sisters and I were strolling down the long aisles when I saw it just off to the left: the toy department... the size of a Super Target.

Seriously.

Now I really can't explain why but when all the Kimball girls went right, I went left and found myself in Matchbox Car Heaven. Hundreds, maybe thousands of the tiny blue and gold boxes lined the shelves, all revving their imaginary engines, calling my name... *"Tommy!"*

But that wasn't all. There were scores of other toys lining the shelves as far as a boy could imagine. Etch-a-sketch was brand new, barely three years old. There were the Mattel Winchester rifles that fired real plastic bullets that I'm sure blinded millions of little boys and girls but no one seemed to care about that back then. If someone pointed a toy gun at you in those days, you were smart enough to duck or close your eyes or shoot back.

Susan, Tom and Alice...

Then there were the sturdiest of trucks and jeeps and tractors...the Tonka Toys. They were beefy metal things, made of steel with sharp edges and solid rubber tires that were so real you could smell the diesel from their imaginary engines. But what distracted me from the company of my family was sighting the ultimate bicycle: a 20-inch Street Series Schwinn Sting-Ray.

This was an amazing machine, looking more like a motorcycle than a bicycle. Complete with a banana seat and high-rise handlebars, The Sting-Ray screamed "cool." A chopper bike for only $49.95? That's not much money, is it? I could ride it to school. I would be the coolest kid in the neighborhood.

I slowly walked over to it, then, all the way around it, afraid to touch it, mesmerized by its sleek body and bright blue color. Gingerly, I grabbed the handlebars and seat and gently nudged the kickstand out of the way. I turned the handles back and forth, the tires squeak-squeaked on the linoleum. I was about to saddle up when a woman's sharp voice brought me back to reality.

"You can't ride that in here, young man! Where's your mother?"

My mother? Where *was* my mother? I turned to see an *I Love Lucy* beehive underscored with a pair of horn-rimmed eyeglasses that dangled from a sequined leash around her neck. The woman wore a nametag, Rose, which made her less scary but not by much. She definitely had thorns.

"Why, she's right here..." I looked up the aisle. No, no mom. "I mean, she's right, uh..." I said, looking in the opposite direction. Nope, not there either. "...oh," I finished. I looked again to be sure, then turned back to Rose. I tried to speak but nothing came out; I couldn't see very well anymore either. I blinked and felt a rush of tears streak down my cheeks and plop onto the toes of my brown leather high-top Thom McAn Shoes. In that moment, I was certain I would never see my family again.

"Aw, poor dear, are you lost?" A Rose by any other name couldn't have sounded as sweet.

I was lost. Lost in Lancaster. I shuddered when I answered her. "Yes, ma'am."

"Well, what's your name, sweetie?" Sweetie? No one calls me sweetie except my Mom. Then, she reached toward me, I'm sure just to comfort me, but when you're lost in a store that's bigger than your neighborhood, the "fight or flight" instincts take over. I was too little and too scared to fight, so, with tears streaming down my face, I instinctively gripped the Sting-Ray, ran the bike down the aisle and toward a huge display of new, red kick balls. Just as I passed the Tonka Toys, I hopped into the banana seat.

Now for those of you who have never mounted a Street Series Schwinn Sting-Ray while running, aside from the alliteration of the name, the other, trickier part about the bike is, steering it. This is significant for a variety of reasons but primarily because there are three actions associated with riding a brand-new Sting-Ray.

First is balance; you have to be able to balance yourself on the bike. I knew how to do this. I'd been riding my bike for, well, weeks, maybe months, but on a wide country lane, not through the toy department at Woolworth's. The second thing is, braking. Again, I learned how to do this on my bike on gravel and macadam, and dirt; not on department store linoleum. Of course, braking was a new, hard-earned technique thanks to the mishap I'd had with a gum tree earlier that summer. Finally, there is the steering. This is critically important on the street but even more so in a store with so many obstacles at close proximity.

Sting-Rays, while really cool to look at and be seen on, weren't, in my humble opinion, really all that user-friendly when it came to steering. My hands on my short little arms were at eye level when gripping the ends of the chopper handlebars. And you know, turning a Sting-Ray? Because of physics you only have to tweak the handlebars slightly in the direction you want to go. Slightly. Turn them too far—like I did—and the front tire bites the linoleum, bucking the rider clean out of the banana seat and into a basket full of kick balls—scattering them everywhere.

When the balls stopped bouncing, Rose stood over me, fussing and talking, helping me to my feet and telling me that I had nothing to worry about. She talked, and laughed—fluttered, really—walking me to customer service and the public address system to announce to everyone in Pennsylvania that there was a lost boy named Tommy who tried to make off with a Sting-Ray and ended up crashing halfway between toys and sports.

I stood there shaking for what seemed to be the longest time, waiting for my mother to claim me. Though she never said she was embarrassed, she didn't have to. Maybe she wasn't. Maybe she was busy taking care of my baby sister. But when Susan, my 18-year-old sister, turned the corner and walked up to me, I was never so happy to see anyone in my entire life.

Rose asked, "Is that your Mother?"

I said, "Yes," loud enough for Susan to hear me. She smiled slyly and put out her hand. I bravely took it, hands still shaking, knees wobbly. She didn't say anything until we had walked a ways.

"You okay?"

I almost lost it. "Yes," I said, nodding.

We walked a little farther down that long, center aisle at Woolworth's. I felt as though an angel had rescued me. I looked up at my big sister again. She looked so tall and brave and beautiful. I craned my neck to check for wings. She noticed and stopped. She knelt down and right there in the middle of that store in Lancaster, Susan gave me the biggest, warmest, best hug I've ever had.

Funny thing about hugs like that: they make you cry like a big baby, which I did. And they make you feel loved, which I did. And they make you realize that family is more important than a whole store full of toys. I sure miss that angel.

Ok, so maybe it didn't happen exactly like that, but that's how I remember it.

Even at the tender age of nine, Susan shows motherly
love and instincts toward younger brother, Tommy.

CHAPTER 15

· · · · · · · · · · · · · · · · · · · ·

Dad's Yellow Dinghy

In spite of his precise nature, my father had a warm and patient heart. He was inordinately patient with his children—especially me.

One time I popped into the workshop while Dad was soldering something. Of course I was chatting away, not really aware of what was going on. So, when I grabbed a handful of the soldering iron held in the bench vice, I was shocked at how hot it was.

I pulled my hand away and watched the skin blister before my eyes. "Ow! That's hot." No kidding, Sherlock. But Dad remained utterly calm.

"Boy," he said, in almost a drawl, "you'd better put some ice on that." That's all he said. There was a lot of meaning in what his compassion didn't say, but kindly implied.

As an engineer and machinist for the Aberdeen Proving Grounds, Dad was a stickler for getting things done right. If you needed to build something and you got sloppy with your measurements, he'd allow that...as long as you were only off by a hundredth of an inch. Precision to my father was measured in thousandths of an inch.

That was how he built the two-story addition to our family home on Lyon Street; how he laid in the solid oak floors that are tight enough to be called seaworthy; how he transplanted azaleas or cut down trees…how he performed any task.

"Do it and do it right with the right tools," he'd say. *Or don't do it at all*—he never said it, but he implied it. And if you decided to do something, it was, "Watch one. Do one. Teach one."

Pop loved sailing. He built his first boat in the living room of the family home on Deaver Street and sold it before I was born. His second was a scale model of a skipjack—a centerboard, bateau design he drew up and built himself, from wood.

Dad grew up around craftsmanship, and although he inherited his father's engineering prowess, he wasn't much for motor craft. "Too noisy, smelly and dirty," he'd say, long before being green was fashionable. "Nothing like letting the wind move you along."

Somewhere in our family tree, there were sailors. Lots of them. How do I know this? Because Dad loved the water, and he loved sailboats, as though they were in his DNA.

He'd often fall into a quiet, reverent recitation of *Sea Fever* by John Mansfield:

I must go down to the seas again, to the lonely sea and the sky,
And all I ask is a tall ship and a star to steer her by,
And the wheel's kick and the wind's song and the white sail's shaking,
And a grey mist on the sea's face and a grey dawn breaking.

I must go down to the seas again, for the call of the running tide
Is a wild call and a clear call that may not be denied;
And all I ask is a windy day with the white clouds flying,
And the flung spray and the blown spume and the sea-gulls crying.

I must go down to the seas again to the vagrant gypsy life,
To the gull's way and the whale's way,
*   where the wind's like a whetted knife;*
And all I ask is a merry yarn from a laughing fellow rover,
And quiet sleep and a sweet dream when the long trick's over.

It was my father's last wish he be remembered thusly. I read that poem at his funeral, as he'd requested; I was weeping seas of tears by the time that trick was over.

His love for sailing and wooden boats never waned. He kept at it until he simply couldn't lift a hammer.

So, you can imagine my surprise when, one sunny, spring Saturday, as Dad was painting our upside-down dinghy a bright yellow in preparation for the Chesapeake Bay that season... I caught him *cursing* the wee boat. I'll explain.

Mom had asked me to go into their bedroom to fetch something—I can't remember what—and when I got into their room, which shared a wall to the carport, I heard Dad talking to someone. Or so I thought. Mom was in the kitchen, so I knew it couldn't be her. My older brother and sister weren't around, and my kid sister was upstairs in her room. So who?

I peered through the open window, expecting to see Dad and one of our neighbors chatting; but he was alone, painting. Actually, he was plucking little bugs off of the fresh, tacky paint, one at a time, naming each one while mentioning its unsavory lineage.

This was the first, and only, time I ever heard my father curse. In fact, he was cussing, as they say, like a sailor. Of course I burst out laughing. He looked up and saw my face in the window and started laughing too.

"Come out here and help me get these little buggers off the boat, Tommy."

"Aye-aye, cap'n!" I shouted.

Most fun I ever had painting anything, at least, that's how I remember it.

Tommy, the young sailor, takes a swing in a boatswain's chair to catch a
breeze while the Yellow Dinghy dries in the summer sun in the background.

CHAPTER 16

· · · · · · · · · · · · · · · · · · · ·

Lightning Bugs & Wiffle Ball Bats

Baseball was what we did all summer in the Upper Heights neighborhood of Havre de Grace, Maryland, when I was growing up. Mr. Mingle's backyard was the perfect diamond for boys our age and he didn't seem to mind much.

Mingle owned the local Five & Dime, and I suppose he expected it'd only help business if he let us play in his yard. After all, his was the only store in town that carried those skinny yellow Wiffle ball bats and the white, plastic Wiffle balls with holes in them that, well, "wiffled" when you threw them.

Marylanders were all caught up in the Baltimore Orioles in those heydays of Boog Powell, Brooks Robinson, and Frank Robinson. At least to us, the 1966 Orioles were the "best baseball team ever in the history of the world!" We all aspired to play for the "Os." What American kid doesn't dream of playing big league baseball?

Maryland summer nights are hot and muggy, so whether you were Boog Powell, Brooks Robinson, or just some kids in rural Harford County, you sweated profusely after just a few minutes. That was particularly true in 1966 for some reason.

Seems like people used to sweat more in those days. I was nine that summer when I ventured into Mingle's yard for our regular evening Wiffle ball game with three of the four Campanelli boys.

Jonathan, Paul, and Michael Campanelli were from a large Catholic family. Their big sister hung out with my big sister. Their youngest brother was too little to play. So the four of us would pair up into teams, usually Paul and Jonathan against Michael and me.

Their dad Danny worked at the Aberdeen Proving Grounds as a civilian government employee, just like my dad. Danny tested munitions and was pretty good at blowing things up. He had the missing fingers to prove it. My dad was a machinist and was pretty good at machining parts. He had all his fingers to prove it.

Danny was a simple man. He loved sports. He adored his beloved Baltimore teams, the Orioles and the Colts. He loved his wife and family. He loved a good cigar and an occasional beer. He loved his home and took good care of it. But most of all, he loved those boys.

And I'm not sure, but I think he loved them more when they were playing ball. He certainly showed that love to me when I got onto his Little League team. I felt like one of the family; another kid with a glove and cap who wanted to do well to make Danny happy.

He taught me a lot about perseverance that summer I played for him. Put me in right field, sometimes left. Always encouraged me and cheered me on. I had a great arm and a good aim; caught pretty well, too. I just couldn't hit. I think I got one base hit my entire youthful career. Struck out more regularly than a nerd trying to get a date with a cheerleader.

When I would trot back to the dugout, dejected, embarrassed, and frustrated with striking out yet again, Danny would always shout encouragement loud enough for everyone to hear.

"Way to go, Tommy! Great swing! You'll hit it next time! Boog ain't got nothin' on you, boy! Let's go team!" What a great lesson in humility and leadership. I've never forgotten it.

Anyway, back to our Wiffle ball game that evening. The

darker the sky became, the darker and more solid the trees ringing Mingle's yard seemed. That's when the lightning bugs slowly began to appear. At first, it was only a few flickerings, like baseball fans filing into the stadium of trees. Then suddenly, there were thousands. The trees were full of them, blinking like slow-flashing Kodak Instamatic cameras. They winked and cheered as we played into the night.

It was my turn at bat as night rapidly closed in on our sandlot-and-grass ballpark. The lightning bugs were out in full force now and hovering low to the ground, clustering along the first base line like insectoid paparazzi.

It finally got so dark you couldn't see the ball until it was nearly across the plate. I watched Vinnie wind up and pitch. Since I couldn't actually see the ball, I listened for the whistle as it homed in on me. I counted silently: 'one-thousand-one, one-thousand-two' and then I swung as hard as I could on two.

Naturally, this technique was flawed. I missed the ball every time. But this time, in the instant I whiffed it, three rogue lightning bugs, either inadvertently or by God's keen design (depending on your worldview), flew directly into the flight path of my bat!

Hitting or squishing a lightning bug—intentionally or unintentionally—leaves a smear of their "fire" on the striking surface, and for a while, the goo retains its glow like gooey, green paint.

When I smacked these unlucky three in mid-flight, they lit up and tumbled through the thick night air like miniature Molotov cocktails ... one toward first, one down the third base line, and one straight at Vinnie. Beautiful.

We were all awestruck in that one Kodak Moment.

Of course the Wiffle ball game was over and, thanks to my creative accident, a new game was born. We must've clobbered a thousand fireflies that night in one of the most memorable fireworks displays I ever witnessed.

It didn't matter about strikes, or outs, or even the rights of bugs; it was about being boys, sweating together, laughing to the point of exhaustion.

Kamikaze lightning bugs, glow-in-the-dark Wiffle ball bats,

and the sweaty boys of summer... images that linger a lifetime in my soul. Life isn't about homeruns; it's about being in the game.

Yeah. That's how I remember it.

Striking out the Mighty Casey... the author on the grounds of Camp Manidokan, 1961.

TOM KIMBALL

· · · · · · · · · · · · · · · · · · ·

Tom Kimball has been telling stories as a professional writer, actor, director, and producer for theatre, film, and television since 1976. Tom also serves in the Air Force Reserve as a chief master sergeant in public affairs. *That's How I Remember It!* is his first book.

CPSIA information can be obtained
at www.ICGtesting.com
Printed in the USA
FSOW02n1745060416
18863FS